Reading Comprehension

Teacher Created Materials
PUBLISHING

Editor in Chief:
Sharon Coan, M.S. Ed.

Art Director:
Lee Aucoin

Project Managers:
Marcia Russell, M.A. Ed.
Maria Elvira Gallardo, M.A.

Designer:
Lesley Palmer

Product Manager:
Phil Garcia

Product Developers:
Creative Services, Inc.
Teacher Created Materials, Inc.

Photo Credits
Corbis—5, 21, 37, 41, 57, 61, 69, 105, 129
Bookmatrix—9, 13, 33, 45, 53, 65, 73, 85, 93, 101, 109, 113
Corel—17, 81, 117, 125

Hemera—25, 49
Clipart.com—77, 89, 121
TCM—29
Iztli Digital—97

Publisher
Rachelle Cracchiolo, M.S. Ed.

Teacher Created Materials, Inc.
5301 Oceanus Drive
Huntington Beach, CA 92649-1030
www.tcmpub.com
ISBN-0-7439-0121-5
©2005 Teacher Created Materials, Inc.
Made in U.S.A.

Table of Contents

Introduction .4

A Rained-Out Trip 5

The Solar System 9

Baking Blueberry Muffins! 13

Earth's Largest Animals 17

Soccer Win 21

Drink, Drink That Milk! 25

Noises in the Night 29

Monkeys Monkey Around 33

Cheerful Louis .37

A Quicker Picker-Upper 41

Getting a Clue About Clouds 45

At the Circus 49

The Truth About Tooth Care 53

Happenings at the Airport 57

Lydia's First Recital 61

Birds of a Feather 65

A Tasty Treat, a Poison. . . and an
Argument? 69

Jonathon's Special Glasses 73

The Busy Life of Honeybees 77

Amazing Salt 81

The Digestive System 85

One Boy's Wish Upon a Star 89

Is It a Kiwi or a Kiwi? 93

It Starts With You! 97

When Is a Bear Not a Bear? 101

The Three Rs .105

Small Girl in a Big Town 109

From an Egg to a Frog 113

How Spring Came to Be 117

Keeping a Cool Head About Fire
Safety 121

Life Among the Chimps 125

The Festival of Colors 129

Comprehension Review 133

Introduction to Reading Comprehension

The lessons in this book will help you learn to understand what you read. Each lesson has a selection to read. Then you work with skills to help you understand what you read. Each lesson ends with a practice activity that helps you see what you know about the selection.

You can use these steps to help you as you work in the book. For each selection, follow these steps.

1. Read the Before Reading questions.

Before Reading

- Do you have brothers or sisters?
- How are you alike or different from your siblings?

2. Think about what you already know about the subject.

3. Read the selection. Use the During Reading questions.

During Reading

- How did the brothers get along?
- How would you feel about moving?

4. Review the selection using the After Reading questions.

After Reading

- Are there more than these kinds of bikes?
- Which kind of bike would you like to have?

5. Summarize and apply the information. Complete the activities in the book.

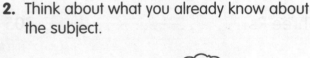

After completing all the activities, use the Comprehension Review section to review the information presented in the book. These pages also help you to check up on your skills.

A Rained-Out Trip

Before Reading

- Read the title. What do you think the story will be about?
- Have you ever been on a camping trip?

During Reading

- Why was the trip canceled?
- What alternative to the camping trip did Dad suggest?

After Reading

- Was the weather forecast completely correct?
- What do you do with your family before you go back to school?

It was the last weekend of summer vacation, and that meant just one thing—the family camping trip! Every year the Lee family went camping on the weekend before school started. Today, the family was driving to the Aleta Fields campgrounds. Mark and Elizabeth had packed up their camping gear the night before and were eager to start the trip. They woke up early and headed downstairs for breakfast.

As soon as they walked into the kitchen, they knew something was wrong. Mom greeted them with pancakes and suggested that they look outside. They could not believe their eyes. It was pouring rain. In their excitement, they hadn't heard the rain beating on the roof or seen it sheeting down the windows. They had paid no attention to anything other than their weekend plans. They had planned to hike, fish, and swim.

They knew that rain meant their camping trip was canceled. With the forecast calling for rain all weekend, the disappointed family wouldn't be doing any camping.

Right then, Dad walked in with a huge smile on his face. "I think we should still go camping, but we'll camp in the family room rather than outdoors. We won't be able to fish, but we also won't have to worry about mosquitoes."

Mark and Elizabeth looked at each other and decided that Dad's idea might actually work. They staked out a camping space in the family room and put their sleeping bags down on the floor. They found their old magnetic fishing game and fished for plastic fish. They helped Mom and Dad rustle up some chili for dinner. They had a good time just being together.

On Sunday, they woke up to a surprise. The sun was shining brightly, and there wasn't a cloud in the sky. Dad said to grab their towels, sunscreen, and bathing suits. They had missed the weekend camping trip, but they could still spend the day at the beach.

Vocabulary

gear: equipment needed for a particular activity

cancel: to call off or stop

forecast: a prediction

magnetic: having the properties of a magnet

Predict

Make predictions as you read. Read the events and questions listed in the chart. Write your prediction about what will happen. Then read the text to find out what actually takes place in the story.

Event	Question	Your Prediction	What Actually Takes Place
Elizabeth and Mark packed up their camping gear.	What will they do with this gear?		
Elizabeth and Mark see the rain.	What do you think their reaction will be?		
It is raining hard.	Will the family go camping?		
The camping trip is canceled.	What do you think the family will do instead?		
Dad suggests that they camp inside the house.	How will the family camp indoors?		
The sun shines on Sunday.	What will the family do now?		

#10121 Reading Comprehension—Level G

Teacher Created Materials, Inc.

Analyze Plot Structure

Complete the chart by analyzing what happened in the story.

Conflict or Problem	
Rising Action	
Falling Action	
Resolution or Outcome	

Comprehension Practice

Circle the letter of the correct answer.

1. Where was the family planning to go?
    A. shopping
    B. amusement park
    C. camping
    D. school trip

2. Why was the camping trip canceled?
    A. Mom had to go to work.
    B. It was raining.
    C. They decided to go somewhere else.
    D. They didn't have their camping gear ready.

3. What did Dad suggest the family do?
    A. forget about camping
    B. watch a movie about camping
    C. go camping anyway
    D. camp inside the house

4. What is a weather forecast?
    A. report of yesterday's weather
    B. prediction of future weather
    C. review of today's weather
    D. information about the climate

5. Why was sunshine on Sunday a surprise?
    A. The forecast had predicted rain all weekend.
    B. It is never sunny after a rainy day.
    C. Sundays are usually cloudy.
    D. Saturday was sunny.

The Solar System

The sun, nine planets and their satellites, and asteroids all make up the solar system. The nine planets revolve around the sun in mostly elliptical orbits.

The nine planets are different sizes, and most have at least one satellite, or moon. Only Mercury and Venus do not have satellites. Look at the chart, which identifies the diameters of the planets and the number of moons each planet has. Which planet is the largest? Which is the smallest? Which planet has the same number of moons as Earth?

Before Reading

- What is the solar system?
- Can you name the nine planets?

During Reading

- Which planet is the biggest in diameter?
- Which planet has the most moons?

After Reading

- Which planets have the same number of moons?
- Which planet is about the same size as Venus?

Planets by Diameter in Miles and Number of Moons		
Planet	**Diameter in Miles**	**Number of Moons**
Pluto	1,423 miles	1
Mercury	3,032 miles	0
Mars	4,194	2
Venus	7,519 miles	0
Earth	7,926 miles	1
Neptune	30,775 miles	13
Uranus	32,193 miles	27
Saturn	74,978 miles	33
Jupiter	88,736 miles	63

Vocabulary

planet: a large object that orbits the sun

satellite: an object that revolves around a planet; a moon

asteroids: very small planet-like objects that orbit the sun

diameter: the distance from one side of an object to the other

Classify/Categorize

Look at the categories given in each chart.

Using the chart from the passage, classify and categorize the planets based on the categories.

Planets with 2 or fewer moons	Planets with more than 2 moons

Planets with diameters less than 10,000 miles	Planets with diameters more than 10,000 miles

Use Text Organizers

Use the chart from the passage to answer these questions.

1. What information does the chart provide?

_____

2. What else would have been useful to provide in the chart?

_____

3. Which planets have no moons?

_____

4. Which planet is about the same size as Earth?

_____

5. Does the chart help you identify the planets in the picture? How?

_____

Draw and label the nine planets.

Comprehension Practice

Circle the letter of the correct answer.

1. How many planets are in the solar system?
   A. seven
   B. eight
   C. nine
   D. ten

2. Which planet is the largest in the solar system?
   A. Pluto
   B. Jupiter
   C. Saturn
   D. Earth

3. Which planet is the smallest?
   A. Pluto
   B. Mercury
   C. Venus
   D. Jupiter

4. Which of the following planets has fewer than 10 moons?
   A. Saturn
   B. Uranus
   C. Neptune
   D. Mars

5. Which of these generalizations is true?
   A. Larger planets don't have any moons.
   B. Smaller planets have fewer moons than the larger planets.
   C. Planets are smaller than asteroids.
   D. Jupiter is bigger than all of the other planets put together.

Baking Blueberry Muffins!

Before Reading	**During Reading**	**After Reading**
• Have you ever helped make muffins or other baked goods? • Why do people use recipe books when baking?	• Why does Sue need measuring cups and spoons? • What does Sue do after she has a creamy mixture?	• What might happen if a baker did not follow the steps of a recipe in order? • Why did Mom check the muffins with a toothpick after 25 minutes?

It was early Saturday morning and Sue woke up excited thinking about the day ahead. Today was the day that she was going to learn how to make blueberry muffins.

"What do you think we need to make blueberry muffins, Sue?" Mom asked. Sue did not respond at first; instead, she found and opened a recipe book to blueberry muffins. Sue read the names of the ingredients and found them with Mom's help. She also found the utensils they needed, including mixing bowls and spoons, a muffin tin, and measuring cups and spoons. Together, Mom and Sue would measure and mix flour, eggs, sugar, salt, baking powder, vegetable oil, milk, and blueberries.

Sue carefully followed all of Mom's instructions. "First, preheat the oven," Mom instructed. Next, Sue measured and combined the dry ingredients in one bowl. In another bowl, she measured and blended the wet ingredients. Then she mixed both together until she had a soft, creamy mixture. After that, she gently folded the blueberries into the mixture.

Sue spooned some of the mixture into each cup of the muffin tin. Then Mom put the muffin pan in the hot oven. Now, all they had to do was wait for about 20–25 minutes for the muffins to bake. Through the glass oven door, Sue watched the muffins rise and brown.

After 25 minutes, Mom tested whether the muffins were done by sticking a toothpick in one. "If the toothpick comes out clean, they're done!" she said.

That morning, Sue and Mom had warm blueberry muffins and milk for breakfast. Sue especially enjoyed her breakfast because it featured her very own muffins!

Vocabulary

ingredient: one part of a recipe

preheat: to allow the oven to heat up before using it for cooking

measure: to find the size or amount of something

mixture: a combination of ingredients that has been stirred together

Identify Sequence

In this story, Sue and her mom bake muffins. Use the chart to sequence the steps they followed for making muffins. The first step has been provided.

Step 1: Find a recipe for the muffins.

↓

Step 2:

↓

Step 3:

↓

Step 4:

↓

Step 5:

↓

Step 6:

↓

Step 7:

↓

Step 8:

↓

Step 9:

↓

Step 10:

Visualize

The author explains that Sue stirred the mixture until it became soft and creamy. Can you picture it? Describe the mixture in the box below.

Mixture

The author also explains that Sue watched the muffins as they baked. In the boxes below, describe the muffins in the tin before and after they baked.

Muffins Before Baking

Muffins After Baking

Comprehension Practice

Circle the letter of the correct answer.

1. What did Sue do first in order to make muffins?
   A. gather the ingredients
   B. find a recipe
   C. preheat the oven
   D. mix the dry ingredients

2. What does <u>combine</u> mean?
   A. to mix together
   B. to bake
   C. to take apart
   D. to separate

3. Which of these would Sue mix with the dry ingredients?
   A. egg
   B. vegetable oil
   C. salt
   D. milk

4. How did Sue's mom test whether the muffins were done?
   A. She used a thermometer.
   B. She set the timer for baking time.
   C. She used a toothpick to test one.
   D. She broke a muffin open.

5. Why did Sue especially enjoy her breakfast?
   A. Breakfast is her favorite meal.
   B. Sue likes milk.
   C. It was a Saturday morning.
   D. Sue made her very own muffins.

Earth's Largest Animals

Have you wondered what the largest animals on Earth are? It depends on where you look. On land, the largest animals are African elephants. What could possibly be larger than an elephant? Well, the blue whale is! Not only is it the largest sea animal, it is even bigger than an African elephant!

While African elephants are the largest land animals on Earth, they are tiny in comparison to blue whales. African elephants can be about 3.5 meters tall at the shoulder and can weigh almost 5.5 metric tons. In comparison, blue whales can be about 30 meters long and weigh about 135 metric tons. That's a big difference! In fact, blue whales are the largest of all animals that have ever lived on Earth.

Both African elephants and blue whales are mammals, which means that the females of both animals produce milk to feed their babies. Mammals are also warm-blooded. The body temperature of elephants and whales remains about the same no matter where they are. All mammals are covered by hair at some point in their lives, although neither African elephants nor blue whales have very much hair. As adults, they just have a few bristles here and there. Mammals also breathe air through lungs. While a whale must come to the surface of the water to breathe, blue whales usually stay near the surface of the water since that is also where their food is.

Both elephants and whales have a good sense of hearing—both can hear low-pitched sounds that humans cannot hear. Although whales have very good sight, they have no sense of smell. Elephants, on the other hand, have poor eyesight and a good sense of smell.

People have used both the blue whale and the African elephant as resources. For example, people have hunted the whale for food and oil. Elephants have been trained to do work and are prized for their ivory tusks. Today, agreements, or laws, protect these giants so that they can continue to live in their natural habitat without facing extinction.

Vocabulary

resource: a supply of something that meets a need

ivory: a hard, white material that makes up elephant tusks

tusk: a very long tooth that is pointed and sticks out of the jaw

extinction: destruction; the state of nonexistence

Before Reading

- What do you think the two largest animals on Earth are?
- What is a mammal?

During Reading

- How much bigger are blue whales than African elephants?
- What is the meaning of "warm-blooded"?

After Reading

- How are African elephants and blue whales alike?
- How are they different?

Ask Questions

You can ask yourself questions and answer them as you read a story. In "Earth's Largest Animals," you read about African elephants and blue whales. You might ask yourself the following questions as you read. Look for the answers in the story.

1. Where does Earth's largest animal live?

_____

2. How much heavier is a blue whale than an African elephant?

_____

3. Why do whales come to the surface of the water?

_____

4. What are some characteristics of mammals?

_____

_____

_____

5. Is an elephant more likely to see or smell an enemy? Explain.

_____

6. Are whales more likely to see or smell hunters? Explain.

_____

_____

7. How have people used elephants as resources?

_____

8. How have people used whales as resources?

_____

Compare and Contrast

Use this Venn diagram to tell how African elephants and blue whales are alike and different.

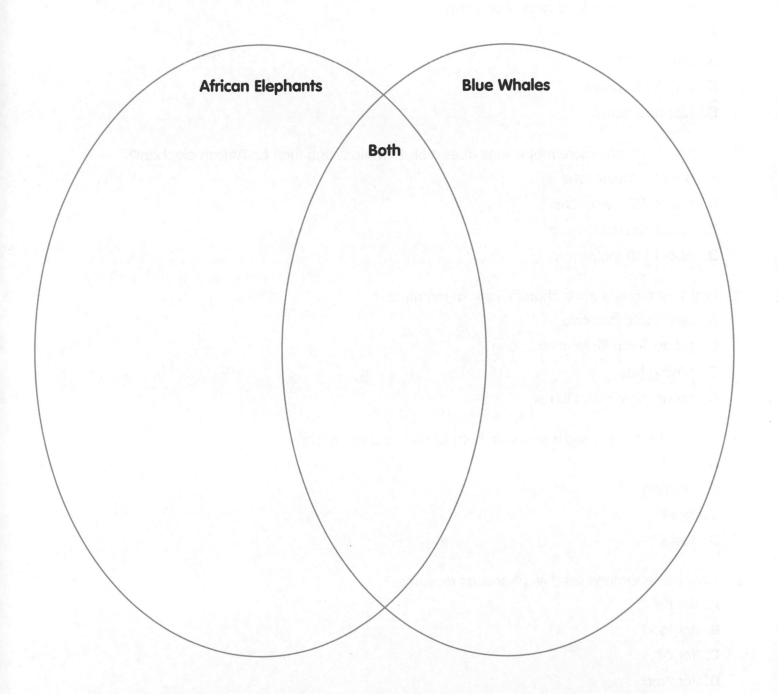

African Elephants   **Blue Whales**

Both

Comprehension Practice

Circle the letter of the correct answer.

1. What is the largest land animal on Earth?
   A. white shark
   B. blue whale
   C. African elephant
   D. hippopotamus

2. About how many more metric tons does a blue whale weigh than an African elephant?
   A. about 2 metric tons
   B. about 25 metric tons
   C. about 100 metric tons
   D. about 130 metric tons

3. Which of these is not a characteristic of mammals?
   A. being cold-blooded
   B. producing milk for their young
   C. having hair
   D. breathing air with lungs

4. Which of these senses is strong in both whales and elephants?
   A. smell
   B. hearing
   C. sight
   D. taste

5. How have humans used elephants as resources?
   A. for fur
   B. for food
   C. for oil
   D. for work

Soccer Win

Saturday is the big championship game, and the fifth-grade soccer team is ready. The team has trained hard all year—they have practiced kicking, stopping, blocking, and shooting the ball. The players have listened to their coach and have carefully followed her instructions. As a result, they remain undefeated this year and are now playing in the championship game.

Katherine and Becky are two of the team's star players. As a forward, Katherine's main job is to score, which is no problem with her powerful and accurate kick. This makes her a strong forward. Becky plays the very tough position of goalkeeper, whose job it is to block the opponent's ball from entering the goal. She is an excellent goalkeeper because she reacts quickly and is not afraid to dive and leap to block the ball. She also has a strong arm for throwing the ball to a teammate.

Katherine and Becky are sure they will win the championship game, but they are trying not to be overconfident. They continue to work hard at practice and to listen to the coach.

On game day, Katherine rushed for the ball as soon as the whistle blew. She passed the ball to Anita, who passed it to Emily, who passed it back to Katherine. Then Katherine moved her feet swiftly, dribbling the ball closer and closer to the goal. Soon she was in position—she shot for the net and scored! Her teammates leaped for joy as they cheered loudly.

The opposing team was also good, however. Katherine and Becky's fifth-grade team led by one point near the end of the second half. With less than a minute remaining in the game, the opponents had the ball. It was up to Becky to save the game. If she blocked the ball from entering the goal, her team would be the champion. But if she didn't, then the other team would win. Becky kept her eyes focused on the ball, looking left to right, right to left, ready to block. Pop! The ball was up, and Becky dove toward it with her arms stretched out. She blocked the shot! The entire team ran toward Becky. They gave each other high-fives and celebrated their victory. They had won the big championship game!

Before Reading

- What kind of sport is soccer? Have you ever played?
- What makes a sports team successful?

During Reading

- What skill is important to be a good forward?
- What made Becky such an excellent goalkeeper?

After Reading

- Why are all positions on a team important?
- Why was the fifth-grade team able to win?

Vocabulary

undefeated: without loss

overconfident: too certain or sure

opponent: the other team in a game; a competitor

Identify Story Elements

Use the chart to identify the story elements. Answer the questions.

Story Elements	
Characters Who is involved? What are they like?	
Setting Where is the action taking place? When is it taking place?	
Plot What is happening in the story? What is the conflict? How is it resolved? How does the story end?	

Identify Cause and Effect

Cause	Effect
	The fifth-grade soccer team is ready for the championship game.
Katherine is a strong and accurate kicker.	
	Katherine's teammates leaped for joy and cheered.
Becky blocked the opponents' final shot of the championship game.	

Comprehension Practice

Circle the letter of the correct answer.

1. Which sport did the team play in the championship game?
   A. basketball
   B. football
   C. soccer
   D. tennis

2. Which of these is Katherine's strongest playing skill?
   A. powerful, accurate kick
   B. good reaction time
   C. moves swiftly
   D. strong throwing

3. What is Becky's position on the team?
   A. defender
   B. goalkeeper
   C. forward
   D. linebacker

4. How many games did the team lose in the season?
   A. none
   B. one
   C. three
   D. all of them

5. Why was Katherine and Becky's team able to win the game?
   A. They were overconfident.
   B. They seldom cooperated as a team.
   C. They worked hard all year.
   D. They had good luck.

Drink, Drink That Milk!

Milk is a favorite drink of people all around the world. Not only is it a popular drink, it is also used as an ingredient in cakes, puddings, sauces, and many other foods. Milk is very important for your health, but it takes many steps to bring milk from the farm to your table at home. Where does milk come from?

Goats, camels, and llamas produce milk that people drink. So do reindeer, sheep, and water buffalo. The type of milk you drink depends on where in the world you live. Most people drink milk that comes from special cows called dairy cattle. Most dairy cattle are black and white and they are raised in very sanitary conditions. People used to squeeze milk from cows by hand, but now milking machines are used. After milk leaves the cow, it has to be kept clean and cool, or else dangerous bacteria will grow quickly.

Milk goes through many stages before you can drink it. First, it is put in a large tank where many tests are done. Next, it is cleaned in order to remove any dust, hair, or dirt that is found.

Then milk production goes through five more important steps. First, milk is divided for different uses. Milk will become either regular milk, cream, butter, or other dairy products. Milk is then heated to a very high temperature to kill any bacteria. This process, called pasteurization, is named for Louis Pasteur, the doctor who invented it.

Next, any fat that may be in the milk is broken up evenly. This prevents the fat from rising to the top. In the fourth step, important nutrients, such as vitamins and proteins, are added to the milk.

Lastly, milk gets put in bottles or paper cartons and gets capped. Special machines are used to cap bottles—some machines can cap 70 bottles in just one minute! Milk is then sent off to different stores and supermarkets, where you probably buy your milk.

Drinking milk is important to the good health of adults and children. Milk helps your body grow and develop and gives you energy. Drinking milk also helps prevent certain diseases. Important vitamins and minerals in milk make your bones stronger. Do you drink enough milk?

Before Reading
- Where does the milk you drink come from?
- Why is milk so popular?

During Reading
- What animals produce milk that people drink?
- What are some important uses for milk?

After Reading
- Why is milk important to good health?
- Why does milk need to be kept cold?

Vocabulary
sanitary: clean; safe to consume

bacteria: tiny living things, some of which are harmful

pasteurization: the process of heating food products to high temperatures in order to kill bacteria

nutrients: vitamins and proteins that keep the body healthy

Develop Vocabulary

Complete the chart by giving the meaning of each word and then writing your own sentence with each word.

Word	Meanings and Sentences
pasteurize	Meaning: Sentence:
divide	Meaning: Sentence:
packaged	Meaning: Sentence:
nutrients	Meaning: Sentence:

Identify Sequence

Sequence is the order in which something happens. In this story, milk goes from the farm to your table at home. What are the steps involved in this process? What is the order of these steps? Tell what happens to the milk at each stage.

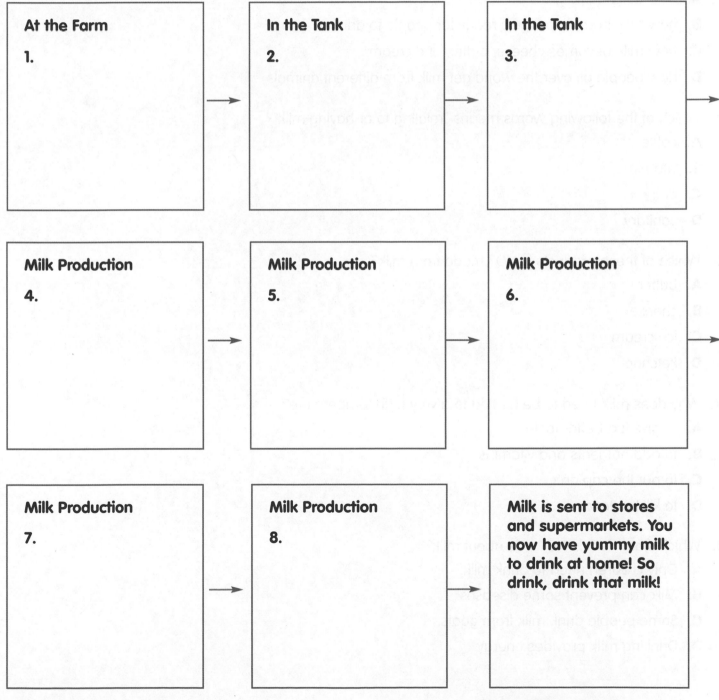

At the Farm	In the Tank	In the Tank
1.	2.	3.

Milk Production	Milk Production	Milk Production
4.	5.	6.

Milk Production	Milk Production	Milk is sent to stores and supermarkets. You now have yummy milk to drink at home! So drink, drink that milk!
7.	8.	

Comprehension Practice

Circle the letter of the correct answer.

1. What process is described in this selection?
   A. how dairy cattle grow on a farm
   B. how milk from a cow gets ready for people to drink
   C. how milk becomes cheese, butter, and cream
   D. how people all over the world get milk from different animals

2. Which of the following words means "relating to or having milk"?
   A. cattle
   B. vitamin
   C. dairy
   D. sanitary

3. Which of these products is NOT made from milk?
   A. butter
   B. cheese
   C. ice cream
   D. ketchup

4. Why does milk need to be heated to a very high temperature?
   A. to give it a better taste
   B. to add nutrients and vitamins
   C. to put the cap on
   D. to kill bacteria

5. Which statement is NOT true about milk?
   A. Only children need to drink milk.
   B. Milk can prevent some diseases.
   C. Some people drink milk from goats.
   D. Drinking milk provides energy.

Noises in the Night

Before Reading

- Are there things that frighten you?
- Would you ever go around your house in the dark?

During Reading

- Where do you think the noise is coming from?
- What kind of boy is Tommy?

After Reading

- Why were the sneakers making the loud noise?
- Why did Tommy fall asleep in the basement?

Tommy was dreaming peaceful dreams. Slowly, he became aware of a noise. It was not loud, really, but it was steady. Tommy woke up suddenly, and his peaceful dream vanished. He sat quietly on his bed, listening. What he thought was a noise in his dream was actually a noise in his house.

"Thump, thump, thump."

What could that sound be? Tommy was an adventurous boy. He needed to know where the noise was coming from, so he got up to investigate. Tommy put on his robe and slippers and grabbed a flashlight.

Tommy headed out of his room, tracking the noise. He headed downstairs, carefully tiptoeing down each step. The living room was dark, and there was no one in sight.

The noise was getting louder, and Tommy could feel his heart beating faster and faster. Tommy used his flashlight to look around the living room. He pointed his flashlight at the front door to check the lock and then at his dog, sleeping quietly in front of the dark fireplace.

"Thump, thump, thump."

Vocabulary

investigate: to take a look or see what happened

amazement: a strong feeling of surprise

relief: the freedom from feeling nervous or worried

exhausted: being very tired

Tommy heard it again, and this time Tommy knew exactly where it was coming from! Tommy took a deep breath and reached for the basement door. When he opened the door, the noise was louder than ever and was joined by a soft humming sound.

"Hello?" Tommy whispered nervously into the darkness. No voice answered, only the continued, mysterious thump-thump-thump coming up from the shadowy basement.

Tommy took a deep breath and then inched down the steps carefully and quietly. As soon as he reached the bottom, he zipped around the corner and pointed his flashlight toward the noise. To his amazement, the noise was coming from the clothes dryer!

Taking a huge gulp, Tommy quickly tugged open the door and found his favorite pair of sneakers! They had become muddy while he played at the park. His mom had washed them and put them in the dryer. Now they were hitting the sides of the dryer and making the loud noise!

Tommy flopped down onto the floor in relief. He suddenly felt exhausted and quickly fell asleep in the quiet basement, tightly holding on to his sparkling-clean sneakers.

Predict

As you read a story, predicting, or guessing, what will happen next will help you to be more interested. Not all predictions will be correct—the story could have a surprise ending.

1. Read the title of the story and stop. What do you think will happen in the story by reading the title?

_____

_____

2. Read the first paragraph and stop. What do you think Tommy will do?

_____

_____

3. Where do you think the noise is coming from?

_____

_____

4. Read through to the seventh paragraph. Now what do you think Tommy will do?

_____

_____

5. What do you think is making the sound?

_____

_____

6. Finish reading the story. How did your predictions compare to what really happened in the story? Was this a surprise ending?

_____

_____

_____

Analyze Plot Structure

The plot is what happens in a story. Fill in the chart below with the events that relate to the structure of a plot.

Conflict (problem or main dilemma)
Rising Action (events that lead up to the climax)
Climax (action is greatest at this point)
Outcome (how the problem is solved)

Comprehension Practice

Circle the letter of the correct answer.

1. Why did Tommy wake up during the night?
   A. He heard his dog bark.
   B. He needed a drink of water.
   C. He was not tired.
   D. He heard a noise.

2. Where did Tommy first think the noise was coming from?
   A. his dream
   B. the television
   C. a car
   D. the dryer

3. Where was the noise really coming from?
   A. the fireplace
   B. outside
   C. the dryer
   D. the chimney

4. Why were Tommy's sneakers in the dryer?
   A. The dog hid them.
   B. His mom put them in to dry.
   C. Tommy put them in to dry.
   D. His mom was playing a trick.

5. Why did Tommy fall asleep on the basement floor?
   A. He likes sleeping on the floor.
   B. He was exhausted.
   C. He was sleepwalking.
   D. He thought it was his bed.

Monkeys Monkey Around

Have you ever been to the zoo? What animals did you see? Have you noticed the monkeys? You should next time! Monkeys are extremely interesting animals.

Monkeys are among the most intelligent and lively animals in the world. Because of their playful nature, monkeys are very popular in zoos, where they are often people's favorite exhibit. There are many types of monkeys—about 200 in all! Most of them live in tropical areas, such as in Central and South America, Africa, and Asia. Many live in tropical forests, high up in the trees. Others live in grasslands called savannas.

Monkeys vary in size, shape, and color. Some monkeys are only about six inches long, whereas the tallest monkeys can be as long as 32 inches. Monkeys that live on the ground have shorter tails than monkeys that live in trees. Monkeys also have differently shaped noses. Some have nostrils that are close together, and others have nostrils that are spread apart. Their eyes are large and face forward, which helps them find food. The number and shape of their teeth also vary. Their hair can be white, orange, brown, gray, or black.

Monkeys have long arms and legs that help them climb trees and run, and their tails help them balance and hang off trees. You may have seen monkeys in zoos swinging from branch to branch using their arms, legs, and tails. It's quite amazing how well monkeys can move from tree to tree. Some can even grab objects with their tails. Monkeys have hands with opposable thumbs and feet with opposable big toes. These opposable thumbs and toes can be used with other fingers and toes to grab even the smallest objects.

Monkeys eat a variety of foods. They usually eat flowers, fruit, grass, and leaves. Lizards, frogs, insects, and birds' eggs may also be part of their diet. Depending on the type of food they eat, the structure of their teeth differs. Those that eat mainly leaves have sharp back teeth to shred the leaves.

Most monkeys live together in social groups, with anywhere from 20 to 100 members. Some even live in family groups. Baby monkeys stay very close to their mothers, who give them food and keep them safe. Monkeys in zoos are lively and always look like they are playing and having fun. This is probably where the phrase "monkey around" came from.

Before Reading

- What are some physical characteristics of monkeys?
- Where do most monkeys live?

During Reading

- What are "savannas"?
- What do monkeys eat?

After Reading

- How do monkeys use their bodies to move?
- What does "monkey around" mean?

Vocabulary

tropical: very hot

opposable: capable of being placed opposite; how the thumb can face and touch the ends of other fingers

structure: the arrangement or organization of things

Summarize and Paraphrase

To summarize and paraphrase something is to give a shorter version in your own words, in a simpler way. In the chart below, summarize/paraphrase each paragraph.

Paragraph	Summarize/Paraphrase
2	
3	
4	
5	
6	

Identify Author's Purpose and Viewpoint

1. What do you think the author's overall impression of monkeys is?

   _____

   _____

2. In paragraph 2, the author writes, "Because of their playful nature, monkeys are very popular in zoos, where they are often people's favorite exhibit." Are monkeys your favorite animal? Do you think they are the author's favorite?

   _____

   _____

3. In paragraph 4, the author writes "It's quite amazing how well monkeys can move from tree to tree." Why do you think the author included this sentence? Does the author think it's amazing that monkeys can swing from tree to tree?

   _____

   _____

4. Pay attention to the adjectives used to describe monkeys in the story. Adjectives are words that describe a thing, animal, or person. Some adjectives in the story include **intelligent**, **fun**, **popular**, and **lively**. Are these positive or negative words? Why do you think the author used these words to describe monkeys?

   _____

   _____

5. Now, what is your overall impression of monkeys? Did you learn anything new about monkeys? What did you learn?

   _____

   _____

Comprehension Practice

Circle the letter of the correct answer.

1. Which of the following statements about monkeys is true?
    A. Monkeys live in Central and South America.
    B. Monkeys live in the forests of Canada.
    C. Monkeys live in tall trees called savannas.
    D. Monkeys live mostly in the zoos of North America.

2. Most monkeys live in what type of climate?
    A. tropical
    B. desert
    C. cool
    D. highland

3. In what ways do their tails help monkeys?
    A. to find food and climb
    B. to fight and stay safe
    C. to keep balance and grab objects
    D. to hold things and chew

4. Of the following, which is a monkey NOT likely to eat?
    A. lizard
    B. fish
    C. grass
    D. fruit

5. Which word describes the ability to grab things with a thumb and fingers?
    A. variety
    B. tropical
    C. savanna
    D. opposable

Cheerful Louis

Louis woke up early Monday morning to get ready for his first day of school. In fact, he was so excited that he didn't even need the alarm to wake him. He practically jumped out of bed and put on his new shirt, pants, belt, and sneakers. Then he sat down to a delicious breakfast that Mom had made. It included all his favorites—orange juice, toast with strawberry jam, eggs, and sausage.

When he was finished eating, Louis put his dishes in the sink. Then he grabbed his baseball cap and his backpack, and he waved good-bye to Mom.

"Have a wonderful first day at school, Louis!" she called after him.

As soon as Louis opened the front door and stepped out, huge drops of rain suddenly started falling. Louis looked up and was surprised to see gray clouds covering the entire sky. The weather forecast had been for a beautiful, sunny day but it was pouring outside! Louis quickly came back inside the house.

Louis needed to do something at once, because the school bus was going to arrive any minute. Louis patiently tried to think of what he could do. Then he put on his raincoat and rain boots and grabbed his umbrella.

With all of his rain gear on, Louis headed out the door again. He was not going to let anything else ruin his first day of school. He carefully walked to the corner where he waited for the school bus. Within minutes, the big yellow bus drove up. As it was coming to a stop, the bus went through a huge puddle and splashed the water right on Louis!

Louis could have been upset about this accident, but instead he put on a smile. "Thanks for waking me up with a splash!" he said to the bus driver. "It's a good thing I was wearing my rain gear."

Most people would have thought that the day was off to an awful start. It might have been enough to put anyone in a bad mood, but Louis is not like most people! He remained cheerful and upbeat. He always loved the first day of school, and he was certain that exciting things were still going to happen on this day.

Vocabulary

forecast: to tell ahead of time what something will be

gear: clothes and equipment for a special activity

ruin: to make something go badly

upbeat: positive, with a good attitude; happy

Analyze Characters

In this story, the author uses certain words to describe Louis and his actions. What do you learn about Louis from the story? What kind of boy is he? Answer the following questions to analyze Louis's character.

1. Read the title. What do you know about Louis from the title?

    _____

    _____

2. What are some of Louis's actions in the first paragraph that let you know he is excited about the first day of school?

    _____

    _____

    _____

3. Imagine that Louis is not cheerful. How would "Uncheerful Louis" react to the rain when he walked out the front door?

    _____

    _____

    _____

4. What can you say about Louis's personality after reading his reaction to being splashed by the bus?

    _____

    _____

    _____

5. What does the author mean by saying that "Louis is not like most people"?

    _____

    _____

    _____

Make Inferences

In this story, Louis's personality is described by showing how he reacted to certain situations. Below are several made-up situations. Use what you learned about Louis and your own ideas to make an inference, or an educated guess, about how Louis might react to each situation. What would you do in each situation?

Situation	How Louis Might React	How You Would React
Louis's mom burns his breakfast.		
Someone at school bumps into Louis and knocks his books from his hands.		
Louis spills juice on his new shirt at lunch.		
A first grader is lost and late because he cannot find his classroom. He comes to Louis for help, but Louis is also late for class.		

Comprehension Practice

Circle the letter of the correct answer.

1. What did Louis NOT have for breakfast?
   A. toast with jam
   B. eggs
   C. pancakes
   D. sausage

2. What kind of weather was Louis expecting?
   A. sunny
   B. rainy
   C. cloudy
   D. windy

3. Which item does not belong in a group with the others?
   A. raincoat
   B. rain boots
   C. sunglasses
   D. umbrella

4. What happened at the bus stop?
   A. The bus driver forgot to stop for Louis.
   B. A puddle of water was splashed at Louis.
   C. Louis left his umbrella there.
   D. Louis waved to Mom.

5. Which of the following words best describes Louis?
   A. positive
   B. rude
   C. angry
   D. silly

A Quicker Picker-Upper

In Joseph's science class, the students were busy working on their projects. They were cutting and pasting all sorts of pictures. Near the end of the day, Joseph needed a paper clip to fasten the remaining materials together. He went up to the teacher's desk to grab one and—crash! Joseph had knocked over the entire container of paper clips!

Joseph groaned. There were so many paper clips scattered about. "It will take me forever to pick all these up!" Joseph said.

The teacher saw the mess and had a great idea. "Students, gather around the front here," Mr. Gorley said. "This is the perfect opportunity to learn about magnets!"

With confused looks on their faces, the students circled the spot with the scattered paper clips. Mr. Gorley pulled out a huge horseshoe-shaped magnet from his drawer. He told the class that magnets can attract, or pull, certain objects made out of metal.

Mr. Gorley held the magnet above the pile of paper clips. He slowly lowered it, and one by one the paper clips were pulled toward the magnet! Soon, dozens of paper clips clung to the ends of the magnet.

Mr. Gorley took the paper clips off the magnet and put them back into the container. Then he handed the magnet to Joseph so he could finish the job. Joseph lowered the magnet toward the paper clips, and in no time the magnet picked up the remaining paper clips.

"Wasn't that easy?" asked Mr. Gorley.

The students had lots of questions about what else the magnet could pick up. Mr. Gorley pulled a box from a nearby shelf. It was full of magnets of many shapes and sizes. He handed one magnet to each student. "Now let's look for more items around the classroom that magnets will attract," said the teacher.

The hunt was on. The magnets stuck to belt buckles, doorknobs, metal rulers, and a stapler. The students had lots of fun learning from the "sticky" problem of some scattered paper clips!

Before Reading

- What do magnets do?
- Where can you find magnets?

During Reading

- How are magnets shaped?
- Why can magnets attract paper clips?

After Reading

- Why would you use a magnet?
- At home or at school, where and how have you seen magnets used?

Vocabulary

fasten: to hold together

attract: to pull objects closer

scattered: spread out; placed here and there

opportunity: a chance; a time

Develop Vocabulary

When you read about some topics, you'll notice that some words that relate specifically to the topic are used. They may have a special meaning when related to the topic that they don't have when you use them to talk about other things. In this story, the topic is magnets. Some vocabulary words are associated with magnets:

1. **attract**—to pull toward

2. **repel**—to push away

3. **pole**—the end of some magnets

Poles that are *different* will <u>attract</u> each other, while poles that are the *same* <u>repel</u> each other.

Fill in the blanks using the three vocabulary words above.

1. A magnet will _____ paper clips.

2. A magnet has two _____ , one "south" and one "north."

3. A north pole and a south pole will _____ each other.

4. A south pole and another south pole will _____ each other.

5. A magnet will not _____ a plastic container.

6. If the ends of magnets repel each other, they must have the same _____.

Use Prior Knowledge and Make Connections

When you read a story, you may find that you already know something about the topic. You can use your prior knowledge to better understand the story and also add on to your prior knowledge if new information is given in the story.

Answer the following questions using your prior knowledge of magnets.

1. At home or at school, how have you seen magnets used?

   _____

   _____

2. What are the different shapes of magnets you have seen or used?

   _____

   _____

3. What objects do magnets attract? What objects do they not attract?

   _____

   _____

4. What are some questions you have about magnets?

   _____

   _____

   _____

Comprehension Practice

Circle the letter of the correct answer.

1. Where does this story take place?
   A. in Joseph's living room
   B. in Joseph's science class
   C. in Joseph's English class
   D. at a science museum

2. What did Joseph need to fasten his materials?
   A. a paper clip
   B. a stapler
   C. tape
   D. a rubber band

3. What did Mr. Gorley use to pick up the paper clips?
   A. a vacuum cleaner
   B. a broom
   C. a magnet
   D. a piece of paper

4. Which object can a magnet attract?
   A. a plastic bucket
   B. a baseball
   C. a coffee mug
   D. a safety pin

5. Why was using a magnet easier than picking up the paper clips by hand?
   A. The floor is dirty, so you would not want to touch the paper clips.
   B. Using a magnet would hurt your hand less.
   C. The magnet could pick up many paper clips at one time.
   D. Paper clips are too small to pick up by hand.

Getting a Clue About Clouds

When you look up at the sky in daylight, what can you see? What color are the clouds? Are they white or are they gray? Do the clouds look fluffy and round or long and feathery? Does it seem as if you could bounce on them just like on a trampoline?

Even though clouds may look soft, fluffy, and bouncy, they are really only a group of small water droplets or tiny ice crystals floating in the air. Clouds are important to the environment. They bring different types of precipitation, such as rain and snow. Without clouds, plants and animals would not get the water they need to live and grow.

There are many types of clouds, and they vary in shape and size. Some clouds stay close to Earth's surface while others form high in the sky. The clouds that are low look like smooth, even sheets. The precipitation that falls from these clouds is usually a drizzle. Middle clouds may also look like smooth white or gray sheets across the sky, or they may form in piles or layers. Rain or snow falls from them.

Some clouds start near the ground but continue up to great heights. Some of these clouds are feathery and thin and look like strands of hair. Others look like enormous chunks of cotton floating in the sky. Others are gigantic dark piles, forming a tall column of cloud in the shape of an anvil, or block. Water crystals form at the tops of these clouds, and they usually bring hail, heavy rain, lightning, and thunder.

For clouds to form, water must evaporate from lakes, oceans, and rivers. Water also evaporates from wet soil and plants—even from your own skin! Water that has evaporated and is in the air is called water vapor. The air with water vapor rises and becomes cooler. Cool air cannot hold all the water vapor, and the extra water vapor turns into tiny water droplets or ice crystals, which form clouds.

Clouds hold a lot of clues about the weather. If you learn to read the clouds, you can probably make some good guesses about the type of weather to prepare for.

Before Reading

- How do clouds form?
- What do clouds look like?

During Reading

- What are clouds made up of?
- What type of clouds bring heavy rain?

After Reading

- Why are clouds important to the environment?
- What are the different types of clouds?

Vocabulary

crystal: a frozen liquid that is clear and has many sides

precipitation: rain, snow, or hail

evaporate: to change from a liquid into a gas

vapor: a gas formed from a liquid

Use Prior Knowledge and Make Connections

Fill in the following chart. First, answer each question with what you already know about clouds—that's called prior knowledge. Then tell what you learned from the selection—that's new knowledge. Write any additional questions you would like answered about clouds.

Prior Knowledge	New Knowledge	Additional Questions
What color are clouds?		
What can come out of clouds?		
How are clouds made?		
Are all clouds the same?		

Visualize

In this selection, shapes, colors, and sizes of different types of clouds are described. Draw and label pictures of each type of cloud. Be sure to include Earth in your drawing as well.

HIGH

MIDDLE

LOW

Comprehension Practice

Circle the letter of the correct answer.

1. What are clouds made of?
   A. water droplets or tiny ice crystals
   B. cotton balls
   C. steam
   D. thick smoke

2. Why are clouds important to the environment?
   A. They are nice to look at.
   B. They block the sunlight.
   C. They bring different types of precipitation.
   D. They bring wind and storms.

3. Which of the following best describes middle clouds?
   A. wet and fluffy
   B. white or gray sheets in layers
   C. feathery and thin
   D. enormous chunks of cotton

4. Which is NOT brought by tall, anvil-shaped clouds?
   A. heavy rain
   B. lightning
   C. thunder
   D. hurricanes

5. What causes water vapor to turn into tiny water droplets?
   A. water evaporating from oceans and plants
   B. cool air that cannot hold all the water vapor
   C. clouds climbing to great heights
   D. clouds that look like smooth, even sheets

                    Teacher Created Materials, Inc.

At the Circus

It was a special day for Jennifer. Her family had tickets to the circus. Jennifer had never been to a circus, so she was very excited.

As they entered the large tent called the big top, a clown came up to Jennifer and asked her to pull the flower on his shirt. When she did, water squirted out of the flower onto the clown's face. Jennifer laughed and shook the clown's hand.

Jennifer and her family found their seats just as a drum roll announced the beginning of the show. During the first act, three clowns entered the ring, which is a round area where the action takes place. The clowns used balls, bicycles, and hoops to perform many tricks. Their childish jokes made the entire audience laugh.

Next, a man entered a different ring with two tigers. Jennifer was worried that the man would get hurt, but her dad told her that the tigers were well trained. The man led the tigers around the wire cage several times. The trainer had the tigers sit on stools and jump through a fire-lit hoop! Jennifer was still nervous, but she enjoyed the thrilling act.

After that, five elephants and two elephant trainers entered a third ring. Jennifer was overjoyed to see her favorite animals. It was amazing to watch the huge elephants stand on top of tiny stools. A lady in a beautiful costume climbed up on top of one elephant. Then the elephant began to walk on its two hind, or back, legs.

The last performers to come out were a high-wire team. The team was a group of men and women who walked on wires high above the ground. The wires were only about as thick as Jennifer's thumb! Some members of the team carried a pole for balance. Others strapped their legs onto ropes and hung upside down, twirling hoops around their arms at the same time. A few of the men and women did many dangerous flips and turns on swings. Jennifer's mom explained that these performers train for many years to learn these tricks.

When the final act was over, Jennifer got up with her parents to leave. The same clown that she had met when they arrived handed her a giant flower made from bright balloons. Jennifer couldn't imagine a better way to spend the day.

Before Reading

- What is a circus?
- What might you see at a circus?

During Reading

- What is a high-wire team?
- What happens in circus rings?

After Reading

- What tricks did the elephants perform?
- What helps some high-wire performers keep their balance?

Vocabulary

audience: a group of people watching a show

perform: to do an action

childish: acting like a child; silly

balance: the ability to stay upright

Summarize and Paraphrase

Rewrite each paragraph of the selection in your own words.

Paragraph	Summary
1	
2	
3	
4	
5	
6	
7	

 #10121 Reading Comprehension—Level G   Teacher Created Materials, Inc.

Ask Questions

As you read, asking questions about what you read helps you learn and remember, and might even spark your interest for future reading! Answer the first three questions about the circus—use any prior knowledge you have or make educated guesses about what the answers are. Then add two questions of your own and look for answers in the story and in other places.

1. How do circus performers and animals travel from place to place?

_____

_____

2. Are all circuses the same?

_____

_____

3. What do members of a high-wire team use to keep them safe?

_____

_____

4. My Question: _____

_____

Answer: _____

_____

5. My Question: _____

_____

Answer: _____

_____

Comprehension Practice

Circle the letter of the correct answer.

1. Why was Jennifer excited about going to the circus?
   A. She loved circus music.
   B. She had a friend performing with the high-wire team.
   C. She had never been to the circus before.
   D. She wanted to join the circus someday.

2. Why did the audience laugh at the clowns?
   A. They were afraid of the clowns.
   B. They thought the clowns' tricks were funny.
   C. The clowns were in the wrong ring.
   D. The clowns did amazing tricks with tigers.

3. Which word best describes how Jennifer felt while watching the tigers?
   A. nervous
   B. relaxed
   C. calm
   D. eager

4. What are Jennifer's favorite animals?
   A. rabbits
   B. tigers
   C. seals
   D. elephants

5. Why did some members of the high-wire team use a pole?
   A. to help them swing
   B. to reach across to the other side
   C. to help them balance
   D. to make the audience nervous

The Truth About Tooth Care

How many times do you brush your teeth a day? Do you eat a lot of sweets? Do you go to the dentist twice a year? These are all important questions to think about if you want to have healthy teeth for life.

Starting at around age five or six, you probably began losing your 20 primary, or "baby," teeth. That is because your permanent teeth were erupting, or coming through your gums. By the time you are 14, you will probably have a full set of 28 permanent teeth. (Four more teeth, called "wisdom teeth," usually come in at around age 20.) After a permanent tooth comes in, you cannot grow a new tooth in that spot. That means it is very important to take good care of the teeth you have!

A cavity, which is a hole in the tooth, forms when bacteria eat through part of the tooth. If the cavity is not filled, it will get bigger and deeper, which can cause pain. There are several things you should do every day to stop the decay and keep your teeth healthy.

One is to brush your teeth at least twice a day, more often if possible. Brushing with a soft-bristled toothbrush and fluoride toothpaste after every meal and after eating any sweet snacks is the best way to guard, or protect, against tooth decay. It is important to clean the front, back, and top surfaces of all your teeth. Brushing your tongue to remove food particles and bacteria is also a good idea.

Another step you can take to protect your teeth is flossing. Floss is a thin thread that can slide between teeth to remove food and bacteria that your toothbrush can't reach.

You can also take care of your teeth by watching what you eat. Eating foods that are high in sugar can lead to tooth decay. That's because bacteria that cause tooth decay love sugar. You can replace sugary snacks with fruits and vegetables, which are good for your body as well as your teeth!

Finally, it is important to visit your dentist regularly. The dentist can give your teeth a good cleaning, check for and fix cavities, and teach you the right ways to brush and floss. Don't ever be afraid to go to the dentist. Having healthy teeth will always give you something to smile about!

Before Reading

- What is a cavity?
- What happens when teeth go bad?

During Reading

- How does tooth decay affect your teeth?
- What can cause a tooth to decay?

After Reading

- What can you do to take care of your teeth?
- What might happen if you do not take good care of your teeth?

Vocabulary

permanent: meant to last for a long time

erupting: breaking through or coming out

bacteria: germs

particles: very small pieces

Develop Vocabulary

When you read a text, there may be words that you do not know. Sometimes, the meaning of a new word is included in the same sentence or in a nearby sentence. Even if the meaning is not clearly stated, you can use other parts of the text to learn what the new word means.

Read the following sentences from the article. Underline the words of the sentences that help you understand what each bold faced word means. The meaning of the word is included in the sentence. Then use the bold faced word in a sentence of your own.

1. Starting at around age five or six, you probably began losing your 20 **primary**, or "baby," teeth.

   My Sentence: _____

   _____

2. That is because your permanent teeth were **erupting**, or coming through your gums.

   My Sentence: _____

   _____

3. A **cavity**, which is a hole in the tooth, forms when bacteria eat through part of the tooth.

   My Sentence: _____

   _____

4. Another step you can take to protect your teeth is **flossing**. Floss is a thin thread that can slide between teeth to remove food and bacteria that your toothbrush can't reach.

   My Sentence: _____

   _____

Identify Main Idea and Supporting Details

The main idea of an article is the most important thing the writer wants the reader to remember. The writer adds facts and details that add to, or support, the main idea. Fill in supporting details from the article for the main idea in the web.

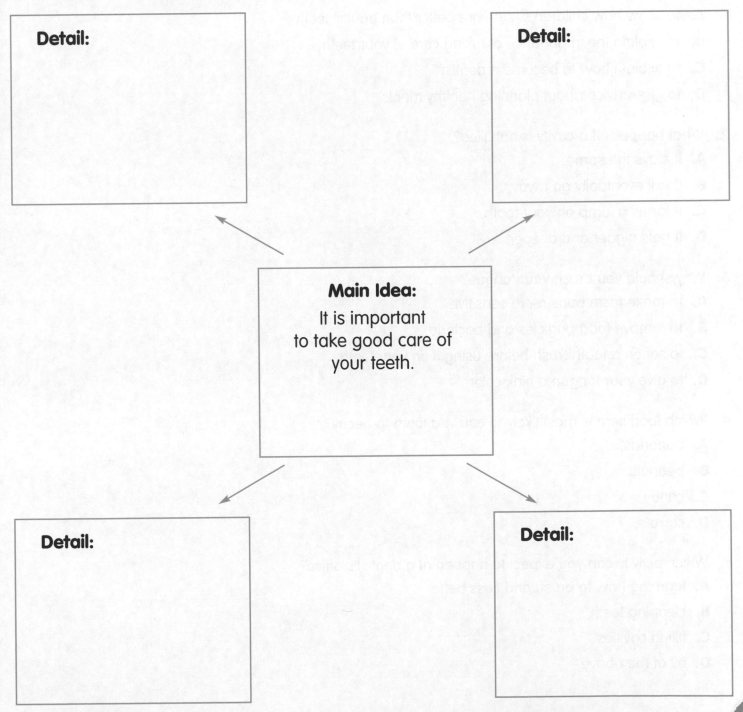

Detail:

Detail:

Main Idea:
It is important
to take good care of
your teeth.

Detail:

Detail:

Comprehension Practice

Circle the letter of the correct answer.

1. What is the purpose of this story?
    A. to show how children's teeth are better than adults' teeth
    B. to explain the importance of taking care of your teeth
    C. to explain how to become a dentist
    D. to give advice about planning healthy meals

2. What happens if a cavity is not filled?
    A. It stays the same.
    B. It will eventually go away.
    C. It forms a lump on your tooth.
    D. It gets bigger and deeper.

3. Why should you brush your tongue?
    A. to make taste buds more sensitive
    B. to remove food particles and bacteria
    C. to soften a toothbrush before using it on your teeth
    D. to give your tongue a pink color

4. Which food item is most likely to cause a tooth to decay?
    A. bananas
    B. peanuts
    C. candy
    D. carrots

5. Which activity can you expect to happen at a dentist's office?
    A. learning how to brush and floss better
    B. cleaning teeth
    C. filling cavities
    D. all of the above

Happenings at the Airport

Before Reading

- Have you ever flown on an airplane? If not, would you like to?
- Why are you supposed to arrive early at an airport?

During Reading

- How could the family have made sure they were not going to be late?
- Why was the family glad to see Grandma and Grandpa?

After Reading

- How would you feel if you missed a plane?
- Was the family's reaction what you would have expected? Why or why not?

Kristina's family was going to visit her grandparents. Kristina was so excited! It had been months since their last visit. They called a taxicab to take them to the airport. "This will save us lots of time," Dad said. "We won't have to worry about parking."

However, the streets were crowded with cars, and the cab slowly made its way to the airport through the traffic. They arrived at the airport very late, got stuck at a checkpoint for a while, and had to run all the way to the gate to catch their plane. Out of breath, they finally reached the gate. The attendant saw them dash up and shook her head sadly. "You checked in too late," the attendant said, "so we had to give your seats to other people. Now the plane is completely full."

The attendant booked them another flight, which would leave two hours later. The family was upset, but all they could do was wait. Mom and Dad were worried now because they were going to be late, and Grandma and Grandpa would have to wait too.

After two long hours, the family finally got on a plane. When they got off the plane after the quick flight and went out to the front of the airport, Grandma and Grandpa greeted them with huge smiles. Mom, Dad, and Kristina were very glad to see them at last, and they couldn't wait to get to their house.

Grandpa took Kristina's hand, and they happily chatted and laughed as they went together to pick up the luggage. They waited and waited, but their luggage was nowhere to be seen! Dad asked an airport worker for help, and she looked on her computer for a minute or two. "I'm sorry, but it seems that your luggage didn't get on your plane," she said. "It won't be here for another hour."

After another hour, the family picked up their luggage and left the airport. The sun was setting as they pulled into her grandparents' driveway. Everyone was starving and exhausted, so Grandpa quickly fixed up a tasty meal that everyone quickly ate. When they were all full and rested, Grandma pulled out a board game, and they played for the rest of the evening. Even though the day was full of mishaps, they were all happily together.

"This is why trips are so much fun!" Kristina said.

Vocabulary

checkpoint: a place where people are stopped and checked for safety reasons

attendant: someone working to help you

booked: reserved

mishaps: small accidents

Analyze Plot Structure

The plot is the action that happens in a story. Fill in the chart below with the events from the passage that relate to the structure of a plot.

Conflict (problem or main dilemma)
Rising Action (events that lead up to the climax)
Climax (action is greatest at this point)
Outcome (how the problem is solved)

Identify Cause and Effect

A *cause* is why something happens and an *effect* is what happens. To find the cause, ask the question, "Why did this happen?" To find the effect, ask the question, "What happened because of this?" In a story, an effect often becomes the cause of another event. Clue words such as **because**, **so**, or **since** can sometimes be helpful in recognizing cause-effect relationships.

Fill in the missing causes and effects in the chart. Then try to add one more cause-effect relationship to the chart.

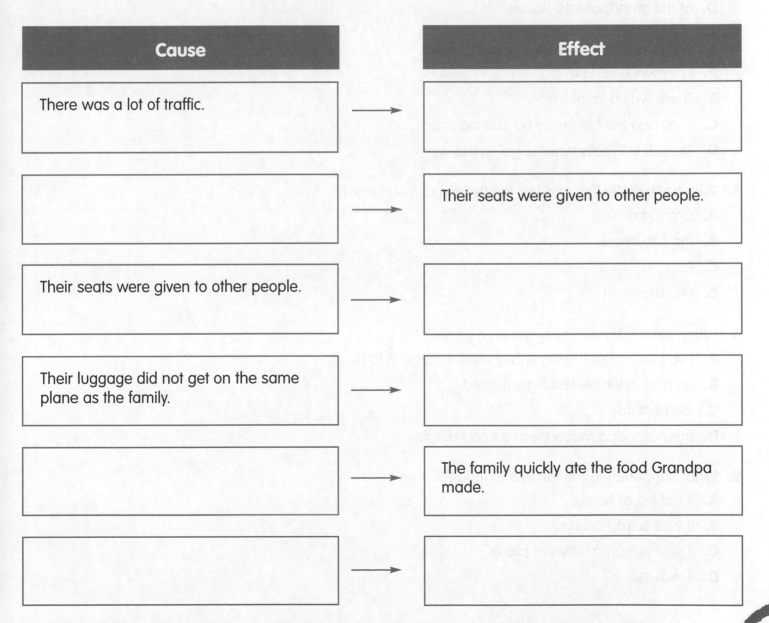

Cause	Effect
There was a lot of traffic.	
	Their seats were given to other people.
Their seats were given to other people.	
Their luggage did not get on the same plane as the family.	
	The family quickly ate the food Grandpa made.

Comprehension Practice

Circle the letter of the correct answer.

1. Where does most of the action in the story take place?
   A. in a cab
   B. in airports
   C. at Kristina's house
   D. at the grandparents' house

2. Why did the family arrive at the airport late?
   A. They woke up late.
   B. There was a lot of traffic.
   C. They had trouble finding a parking space.
   D. They didn't really want to go on this trip.

3. Who booked Kristina and her family on a different flight?
   A. Grandma
   B. the cab driver
   C. Dad
   D. the attendant

4. When did the family finally get on a plane?
   A. two hours after the flight they were supposed to be on
   B. an hour after the first flight landed
   C. the next day
   D. after Grandpa made them a good meal

5. What happened to the family's luggage?
   A. It got left at home.
   B. It was scratched up.
   C. It was put on a different plane.
   D. It was stolen.

Lydia's First Recital

Lydia began taking piano lessons when she was just four years old. Even then, with her tiny fingers, Lydia tried her best to strike the right keys on the big piano. She loved the beautiful sounds that were made when she touched the white and black keys.

Now she was six years old, and Lydia was preparing for her first recital! Her piano teacher had picked the perfect song. Lydia and several other children would each play a song in front of their families and friends. Lydia practiced for almost two hours every day. She sat at the piano and played the music over and over again! It was hard work, but Lydia didn't mind.

On the day of the recital, Lydia's mom helped her choose just the right clothes to wear. Lydia wanted to be dressed in something special. She put on her new dress and shiny shoes. Her mom fixed her hair with pretty clips.

"Are you ready, Lydia?" Mom asked gently.

"Mom, I'm worried! I have butterflies in my stomach. I don't think I can play in front of that audience," Lydia replied nervously.

Lydia's mom told her to forget about the audience and pretend that she was just practicing. She thought this would help Lydia to relax. Then her mom gave Lydia a big hug and told her that she would be great.

Lydia was the third student to perform. When it was her turn, she slowly walked onto the stage and faced the audience, but all she could see were bright lights. She really could pretend she was just practicing! Lydia looked back at her mom, who gave her a thumbs-up sign. This made Lydia feel more comfortable and confident. She bowed and walked over to the piano.

How wonderful the music sounded, just like when Lydia played the piano at home! Lydia's little fingers moved smoothly over the piano keys, and she smiled the whole time. Lydia did a great job!

When she finished, Lydia stood up and faced the audience again, but this time she wasn't nervous. The people in the audience gave her a big round of applause. Lydia turned to see her mom, and they smiled at each other. Lydia had successfully finished her first piano recital! With newfound confidence, Lydia couldn't wait until the next recital.

Before Reading

- What does it take to become good at playing an instrument?
- What situations make you nervous?

During Reading

- Why do you think Lydia was so nervous?
- What does it mean to have "butterflies in your stomach"?

After Reading

- How did Lydia's mom help her feel more confident?
- How did *not* seeing the audience help Lydia?

Vocabulary

recital: a show given by dance or music students

confident: feeling that you can do something

successfully: having the result you wanted or expected; to do something well

newfound: recently, or newly, found or discovered

Identify Cause and Effect

Remember that a **cause** is why something happens and an **effect** is what happened. Read the following sentences from the story. Identify the cause and the effect for each by writing them in your own words on the lines.

1. On the day of the recital, Lydia's mom helped her choose just the right clothes to wear.

   Cause: _____

   Effect: _____

2. "I have butterflies in my stomach. I don't think I can play in front of that audience."

   Cause: _____

   Effect: _____

3. Lydia looked back at her mom, who gave her a thumbs-up sign. This made Lydia feel more comfortable and confident.

   Cause: _____

   Effect: _____

4. Lydia had successfully finished her first piano recital! With newfound confidence, Lydia couldn't wait until the next recital.

   Cause: _____

   Effect: _____

Make Inferences

When you make an inference, you use both reason and information that you know. Answer the following questions, reflecting on the story.

1. What can you infer about Lydia's personality and ability?

_____

_____

2. What can you infer about how Lydia's mom felt about Lydia playing in her first recital?

_____

_____

3. Why was Lydia able to successfully finish her first recital?

_____

_____

4. Why did Lydia feel so good after she finished playing?

_____

_____

5. What can you infer about different ways to perform well at a recital?

_____

_____

Comprehension Practice

Circle the letter of the correct answer.

1. What musical instrument does Lydia play?
   A. violin
   B. flute
   C. cello
   D. piano

2. What was Lydia preparing for?
   A. a recital
   B. a competition
   C. a lesson
   D. dinner

3. How did Lydia know she was nervous?
   A. Her throat was getting dry.
   B. She had butterflies in her stomach.
   C. Her legs were shaking.
   D. She was hungry.

4. How did Lydia's mom signal to Lydia that she would do well?
   A. She gave Lydia a high five.
   B. She smiled at Lydia.
   C. She gave Lydia a thumbs-up sign.
   D. She cheered for Lydia.

5. Which of the following words best describes how Lydia felt when she finished playing?
   A. worried
   B. energetic
   C. troubled
   D. confident

Birds of a Feather

Before Reading

- What birds have you seen near your home?
- Do all birds fly?

During Reading

- Why do birds migrate?
- What is the largest bird?

After Reading

- Why is an ostrich able to run so fast?
- How do feathers help birds?

You have probably seen ordinary birds in your neighborhood and unusual birds at the zoo. There are more than 9,000 types of birds in the world today, and they are found just about everywhere. Birds live in cities and forests. They also live in deserts, on islands, mountaintops, and farms. While all birds hatch from eggs and have feathers and wings, not all birds can fly.

There and Back Again: In some parts of the world, birds leave their homes during certain seasons. In places where it becomes extremely cold and snowy, or too dry or too wet, birds must migrate or they would starve. Most birds migrate in a north-south direction. For example, birds that live in Canada and the northern United States may fly as far south as tropical South America to avoid the winter.

However, not all birds need to leave their homes in cold weather. Some types of birds can survive the winter by eating tree buds, dry berries, and seeds. Examples of these birds are cardinals, sparrows, and finches. Other birds that remain in cold climates live off of young insects and insect eggs. These are usually small birds such as chickadees and nuthatches. Birds that live on mountain tops, such as ravens and mountain quail, just move down into the valley, where it is warmer.

Fine Feathered Friends: The part of the bird that allows it to fly is its wings. All birds have feathers on their wings, and these feathers give wings their shape. Feathers look solid, but actually they are not. They have a shaft in the center that is hollow. Birds have two types of feathers—contour feathers, which are long, and down feathers, which are shorter. Although feathers are sturdy, they do wear out. Birds shed their feathers at least once a year. The process of losing feathers and growing new ones is called molting. Besides helping most birds to fly, feathers also keep birds warm and provide coloring. Certain colors help birds hide from their enemies.

Getting Around: When birds are on land, they move by hopping, walking, and running. Some birds even climb trees in search of insects. The ostrich is not only the largest bird; it is also the fastest flightless bird. Ostriches use their wings for balance, and their extremely long legs allow them to run up to 40 miles per hour. The penguin is another flightless bird that uses its wings, in this case to help it swim.

Vocabulary

migrate: to move from one place to another

tropical: near the equator; hot and humid

shed: to cast aside (as an animal's covering)

hollow: having empty space inside

Use Text Organizers

Use the headings from the passage to answer these questions.

1. What are headings?

_____

2. Migration is when birds leave their home in one area to go to another place during harsh weather. Birds usually migrate to the same areas every year. Under which heading would you expect to read about migration?

_____

3. What information is given under the heading "Fine Feathered Friends"?

_____

4. How would you expect the information in the section titled "Getting Around" to be different from information in the section titled "There and Back Again"?

_____

_____

5. Different headings for these sections might be "Migration, Feathers," and "Other Ways Birds Move". How are these headings different from the ones the author used? Do you like them more or less than the ones in the article? Explain your answer.

_____

_____

_____

Identify Main Idea and Supporting Details

Complete the chart by identifying the main idea and supporting details of each paragraph.

Paragraph	Main Idea	Supporting Details
1		
2		
3		
4		
5		

Comprehension Practice

Circle the letter of the correct answer.

1. Which of the following statements about feathers is NOT true?
   A. Feathers keep birds warm.
   B. Feathers give wings their shape.
   C. Feathers are thick and solid.
   D. Feathers help some birds stay safe.

2. What is "molting"?
   A. traveling from one location to another to find food
   B. using wings to balance
   C. using wings to swim
   D. the process of losing feathers and growing new ones

3. What are two types of feathers?
   A. hollow and solid
   B. ordinary and unusual
   C. down and contour
   D. chickadees and nuthatches

4. How do some birds survive winter?
   A. by moving into valleys
   B. by molting their feathers
   C. by living on mountaintops
   D. by building smaller nests

5. What do penguins and ostriches have in common?
   A. They are both fast runners.
   B. They are both flightless birds.
   C. They are both great swimmers.
   D. They both migrate to South America.

A Tasty Treat, a Poison . . . and an Argument?

Can you imagine a vegetable that can be made into a delicious filling for a pie or can be a poison? That's exactly the case with a vegetable called rhubarb. This sounds amazing, but it's true!

Rhubarb is often mistaken for a fruit because it is usually baked in a pie and eaten as a dessert. In fact, another name for rhubarb is pieplant. When rhubarb is combined with strawberries, raspberries, and apples, the flavor only gets better. Rhubarb is sold in supermarkets in several ways. It comes in fresh stalks, frozen packages, or cans.

The rhubarb plant has large, green leaves on long, thick stalks. Some leaves are as large as two feet across. The stalks may be about an inch wide and can grow up to two feet long. The part of the rhubarb plant that people can eat is the red, juicy stalk. Eating the leaves may make someone ill—they contain oxalic acid, which is a poison.

The leaves of a rhubarb plant appear early in the spring. In cold climates, rhubarb is often the first sign of spring. Sometime later the plant produces large flowers and seeds. Unlike most vegetables, the seeds from a rhubarb plant are not usually used to grow new plants because the seed does not always grow into exactly the same kind of plant it came from. To grow a new rhubarb plant, farmers cut pieces of the root and the buds. Then they plant that part in the ground. That way, the farmer knows that the new rhubarb plant will be similar to the plant from which it was cut. A rhubarb plant can live for five to eight years.

Rhubarb grows in Europe and the United States, but it originally came from Mongolia, an area in eastern Central Asia. Marco Polo, an Italian trader and traveler who journeyed to China from about 1270 to 1290, even mentioned rhubarb in his journals.

Today, the word rhubarb has several meanings. Dictionaries first define rhubarb as "an edible plant." Then the slang definition is given—"a heated argument, squabble, or fight." One dictionary even links the word rhubarb to baseball. It means "the sparks that fly between an umpire and a pitcher when they disagree."

Before Reading

- What is rhubarb?
- Who was Marco Polo?

During Reading

- Which part of the rhubarb plant is safe to eat?
- How are rhubarb seeds unusual?

After Reading

- Why should someone cooking fresh rhubarb be careful?
- Why is pieplant a good name for rhubarb?

Vocabulary

stalk: the main stem of a plant that acts as a support

edible: able to be eaten

slang: an informal way to express an idea

squabble: a noisy argument

Develop Vocabulary

Use the story content to help identify the meaning of each word. Then write your meaning and the dictionary meaning of each word.

Selection Word	What I think the word means	What the dictionary says the word means
fruit		
vegetable		
poison		
climate		
bud		
umpire		

Use Prior Knowledge and Make Connections

Answer these questions about the selection.

1. What is the topic of the selection?

   _____

   _____

2. What fruits are you familiar with that are baked in pies? Have you ever eaten a pie made with a vegetable filling?

   _____

   _____

3. What else do you know about Marco Polo? How did you learn this? If you didn't know anything about him, what else would you like to know?

   _____

   _____

4. What words do you know and use that are considered slang?

   _____

   _____

5. Have you ever been warned to stay away from certain things because they are poisonous? What are they?

   _____

   _____

Comprehension Practice

Circle the letter of the correct answer.

1. Which part of the rhubarb plant is poisonous?
   A. the juicy, red stalk
   B. the seeds
   C. the large, green leaves
   D. the thick roots

2. Which is NOT a way that rhubarb is sold in supermarkets?
   A. fresh
   B. canned
   C. frozen
   D. dried

3. Where was rhubarb first grown?
   A. Europe
   B. Mongolia
   C. United States
   D. Italy

4. What is a slang meaning of rhubarb?
   A. a squabble
   B. something edible
   C. an umpire
   D. a fruit

5. How are new rhubarb plants usually grown?
   A. from the leaves
   B. from the stalk
   C. from the root
   D. from the seeds

#10121 Reading Comprehension—Level G   Teacher Created Materials, Inc.

Jonathon's Special Glasses

Before Reading

- Do you know anyone who wears glasses?
- Why do some people need to wear glasses?

During Reading

- In what way were Jonathon's glasses remarkable?
- What did Jonathon want to do with his special powers?

After Reading

- Did Jonathon really have special powers?
- What would you do if you had special powers?

Jonathon was cheerless when the school nurse first told him that he probably needed glasses. He was even more unhappy a week later at the eye doctor's office. Jonathon sat stiffly with a glum look on his face. His mom was by his side.

"Mom, I really don't want to wear glasses," complained Jonathon.

"But Jonathon, didn't anyone tell you? These are not ordinary glasses. These are special glasses," interrupted Dr. Butler.

Jonathon became excited when he heard that his glasses were unusual. The doctor made it clear that when Jonathon put on these glasses, he would be able to do extraordinary things. He also explained that Jonathon's new glasses would allow him to see in a remarkable way.

Jonathon was curious. Now he couldn't wait to try on his new glasses. The moment that he put them on, Jonathon knew that these were no ordinary glasses. Suddenly, everything became clearer and Jonathon felt different.

On the way home, Jonathon's mom stopped the car at a red light. Jonathon blinked at the light, and it turned green! When they arrived home, he blinked at the lock on the door, and "click," the door opened! Jonathon started having fun with his exceptional glasses. He just glanced at the refrigerator and knew what was inside. He blinked at the television screen and it turned on by itself.

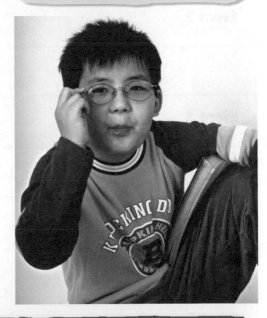

Jonathon went outside to try out his new powers. He hoped that he could help someone. As he was walking down the street, Jonathon noticed a cat stuck high up in a tree. He knew what he had to do! Jonathon simply blinked at the tree, and the tree shrunk. Now it was small enough so that Jonathon could reach up and bring the cat down safely. The glasses were truly amazing!

But then suddenly, Jonathon began feeling dizzy. Had he been overusing his powers? Was he going to lose these amazing abilities already?

"Noooo . . . I can't be losing my special powers. The world needs me to save people!" screamed Jonathon.

"Jonathon, Jonathon, wake up!" his mom said as she shook him gently. "Are you having a bad dream? You need to get ready for your appointment with Dr. Butler. You're getting your new glasses today."

Vocabulary

glum: sad and gloomy

interrupt: to disturb someone who is busy

curious: eager to know about something

overuse: to use something too much

Identify Sequence

Sequence is the order in which events happen in a story. Put the following events in the correct sequence.

Jonathon's mom wakes him up.

The television turns on by itself.

The school nurse tells Jonathon that he needs glasses.

Jonathon starts feeling dizzy.

Dr. Butler tells Jonathon that his glasses are not ordinary.

Jonathon helps a cat down from a tree.

Event 1

Event 2

Event 3

Event 4

Event 5

Event 6

Summarize and Paraphrase

Summarizing and paraphrasing is retelling a story in your own words. Write a summary of "Jonathon's Special Glasses" by answering the following questions. The summary should be written in paragraph form.

1. What did the school nurse tell Jonathon that he needed? Where would he have to go to get it?

_____

_____

2. What was special about the item Jonathon received?

_____

_____

3. What did Jonathon do with the item?

_____

_____

4. What suddenly happened to Jonathon?

_____

_____

5. How does the story end?

_____

_____

Write your summary here:

_____

_____

_____

_____

_____

_____

_____

_____

Comprehension Practice

Circle the letter of the correct answer.

1. Which of the following words best describes how Jonathon felt about getting glasses?
   A. thrilled
   B. unhappy
   C. worried
   D. lucky

2. What did Dr. Butler tell Jonathon about the glasses?
   A. They were lightweight.
   B. They would change the color of his eyes.
   C. They would protect his eyes from the sun.
   D. They were not ordinary.

3. What did Jonathon NOT do with his special powers?
   A. save a cat stuck in a tree
   B. blink at the sky and make it snow
   C. change the red light to a green light
   D. see inside the refrigerator when the door was closed

4. Why did Jonathon want to keep his amazing abilities?
   A. He wanted to save people.
   B. He wanted to brag to his friends.
   C. He saw another cat stuck in a tree.
   D. He liked the way he looked with the glasses on.

5. Did Jonathon's glasses really have special powers?
   A. Yes, they were magical glasses.
   B. Yes, the doctor was a magician.
   C. No, Jonathon was only dreaming about magical glasses.
   D. No, the doctor was only telling Jonathon a make-believe story.

The Busy Life of Honeybees

Although there are about 20,000 kinds of bees in the world, honeybees are the most useful to people. They produce honey, which people use as food. They also produce beeswax, a substance that is used to make candles, crayons, and makeup.

Honeybees are social bees that live in groups called colonies inside hives. A hive might be a box or a hollow tree. The central structure of the colony is the wax comb, which is made up of six-sided, white wax chambers, or rooms. Some honeybee colonies have as many as 80,000 members. There are usually three types of bees in a colony—a queen, workers, and drones—and each type has a specific role to perform.

The queen's only job is to lay eggs. In the spring, the queen lays about 2,000 eggs a day! Each colony has only one queen, who may live for up to five years. If the old queen disappears or becomes feeble, a new queen is made. Sometimes a young queen fights with an old queen until one stings the other to death.

A drone's job is to mate with the queen. There can be up to 500 drones in each colony. Drones are not able to hunt for food because their tongues are too short to suck up nectar from flowers. So they depend on worker bees to feed them. Drones live in the hive in the summer, but in the winter, worker bees may kick them out of the hive if there is not enough food.

Worker bees neither lay eggs nor mate. They spend their entire lives performing duties, or jobs. There are thousands of workers in a colony. At the beginning of their lives, workers clean the hive and feed other bees. Then they produce wax and build honeycomb cells. Later, they protect the hive and eventually hunt for food. Workers hunt for food by sucking up nectar from flowers with their long tongues. Back in the hive, workers put the nectar in an empty cell, where it changes into honey. A worker bee can live for anywhere from six weeks to several months.

People thousands of years ago ate honey that they stole from hives. Today, farmers keep hives of bees and sell the honey. Beekeepers have learned to handle their bees carefully. They wear special clothing, including veils to protect their faces. Thanks to the busy lives of bees, we can enjoy the sweet taste of honey and the fresh scent of candles.

Before Reading

- Have you ever seen a bee in a flower? What was it doing?
- Why are bees important?

During Reading

- What are the different types of honeybees?
- What are the jobs of worker bees?

After Reading

- How do beekeepers protect themselves from bees?
- What useful things are made from beeswax?

Vocabulary

substance: a material, a thing

structure: something built, such as a house

mate: to produce young

nectar: a sweet liquid inside flowers that bees use to make honey

Identify Main Idea and Supporting Details

The main idea is what a story is about. Supporting details are pieces of information that expand on the main idea. Complete the following web by writing supporting details in the outer boxes.

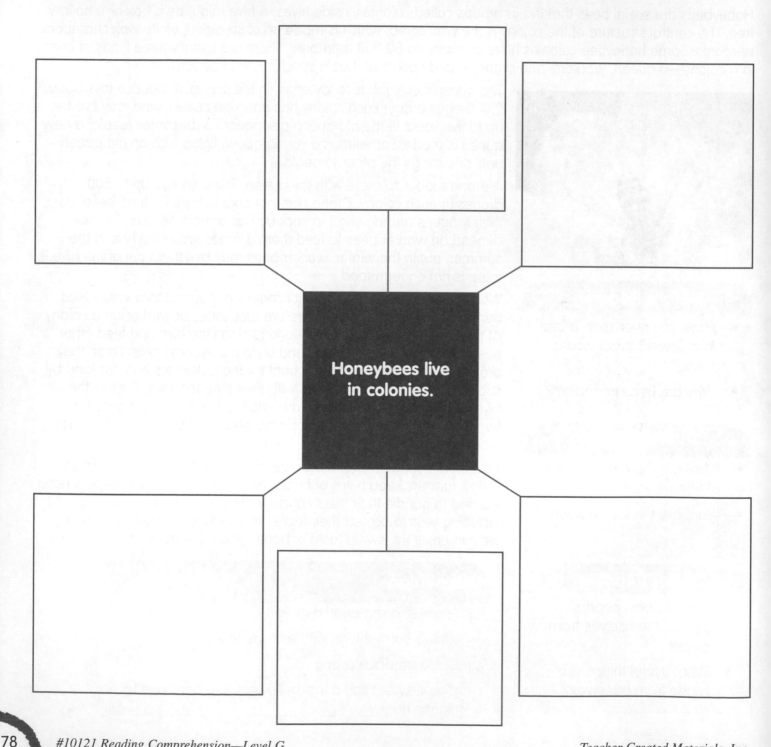

Honeybees live in colonies.

Compare and Contrast

Compare the following types of honeybees.

Types of honeybees	Alike	Different
Queen/Drone		
Drone/Worker		
Worker/Queen		

Comprehension Practice

Circle the letter of the correct answer.

1. Which product is NOT made from beeswax?
   A. crayons
   B. makeup
   C. candles
   D. honey

2. What is the queen's only job?
   A. to protect the hive
   B. to lay eggs
   C. to take care of the young
   D. to protect the drone from worker bees

3. Why do drones depend on worker bees to feed them?
   A. They have short tongues and cannot suck up nectar.
   B. Drones have a higher status than worker bees.
   C. Drones defend the hive, so they cannot hunt for food.
   D. The queen orders the worker bees to feed the drones.

4. Which statement about honeybees is FALSE?
   A. There are usually three types of honeybees in a colony.
   B. Worker bees live as long as people.
   C. Honeybees are social.
   D. All colonies have only one queen.

5. Which word means the sweet liquid inside flowers that bees use to make honey?
   A. colony
   B. chamber
   C. nectar
   D. hive

     Teacher Created Materials, Inc.

Amazing Salt

Christina had to wait an extra twenty minutes to get picked up from school. Dad told her that traffic was bad because people needed to drive slowly due to the snow. Snow had been falling for the past two hours, and the roads were icy and snowy. As the car moved down the street little by little, Christina noticed a big truck ahead of them. The truck was spreading bits of white balls, which Christina did not recognize, onto the street.

"Dad, what is that truck sprinkling on the road?" asked Christina.

"The truck is spreading salt," Dad started to explain.

Christina was confused. Why would a truck be spreading salt on the road? Salt is a seasoning that Christina adds to her food sometimes!

Dad laughed and told Christina that salt is used to season food, but it is also used to melt snow. Snow does not melt easily in cold weather, but salt makes the snow melt at lower temperatures. That is why when there is a snowstorm, special trucks spread salt on the roads. The salt melts the snow and ice, providing better road conditions for drivers. Dad was careful to explain that what was being used on the road was not table salt and should not be eaten. He also told Christina that he uses salt at home to melt the snow on their driveway and sidewalk. He does this to prevent anyone from slipping and falling.

"So salt adds flavor to food and is used to promote safety!" added Christina.

Christina was amazed at these two different uses of salt. Later that night, she decided to learn more about this interesting mineral. She looked up salt in the encyclopedia and learned that salt deposits are underground and that salt is taken out of the ground by mining. Salt is also removed from seawater. When the water from seawater is evaporated, salt is left behind.

She continued to read and discovered that salt has been used since ancient times. It was so important that people used it like money, and many of the first roads and trade routes were created to transport salt. Salt was used to preserve food to keep it fresh and safe. It was even used to preserve Egyptian mummies. Today, salt is used to produce chemicals that make glass, soap, paper, plastic, and cleaning fluids!

"I have a lot to think about the next time I reach for the salt shaker!" Christina thought.

Before Reading

- Does it snow where you live?
- How do you use salt in your home?

During Reading

- What made Christina become interested in salt?
- How does salt melt snow?

After Reading

- Where is salt found?
- How was salt used in ancient times?

Vocabulary

seasoning: something used to add flavor to food

mineral: a natural substance found in the ground

evaporate: to change from a liquid to a vapor

preserve: to make sure something lasts

Identify Cause and Effect

The **cause** is why something happens and the **effect** is what happens. To find the cause, ask the question, "Why did this happen?" To find the effect, ask the question, "What happened?"

Pairs of sentences are given. Identify each sentence as the cause or effect for the pair. A sentence in the first pair has been done for you.

1. Christina had to wait an extra twenty minutes to get picked up from school.

   __Effect__

   People were driving slowly because of the snow.

   _____

2. Salt is sprinkled on the roads.

   _____

   Snow melts more quickly.

   _____

3. Salt was important to people in ancient times.

   _____

   Roads were created to transport salt.

   _____

4. Dad sprinkles salt on the sidewalk.

   _____

   People do not slip or fall.

   _____

5. Christina looked up salt in the encyclopedia.

   _____

   She was interested in learning about salt.

   _____

Ask Questions

Reread the story. Stop and think of questions about salt that you would like answered. An example is done for you, and a question is given for you to answer. After answering the question, write and answer three of your own questions.

	Question	Answer
1.	Why is salt sprinkled on snow?	Salt causes snow to melt at a lower temperature so roads and sidewalks are safer for driving and walking.
2.	How is salt taken out of the ground?	
3.		
4.		
5.		

Comprehension Practice

Circle the letter of the correct answer.

1. Which word describes a substance found naturally in the ground?

   A. preserve

   B. evaporate

   C. mineral

   D. seasoning

2. Why was salt being sprinkled on the road?

   A. to season the street

   B. to help melt the ice and snow

   C. to mine the salt

   D. to preserve the road

3. How does salt help melt snow?

   A. Salt causes the snow to melt at lower temperatures.

   B. Salt changes the snow to a liquid through evaporation.

   C. The white color of salt blends in with the snow and melts it.

   D. Salt turns into ice and melts the snow.

4. Which of the following is NOT a use for salt today?

   A. to trade like money

   B. to keep sidewalks safe

   C. to make soap and paper

   D. to add flavor to food

5. Which word is the process by which salt is removed from seawater?

   A. transportation

   B. preservation

   C. mining

   D. evaporation

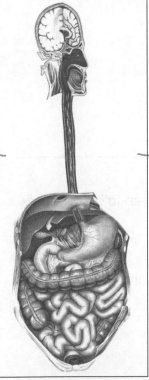

The Digestive System

You wake up each morning hungry. You sit down for breakfast and begin to eat. Have you ever wondered what happens to the food after you eat it? Where does it go, and how does it give you energy and strength?

The human body has a special system of organs that it uses to break down food into smaller pieces. These organs include the mouth, esophagus, stomach, small intestine, and large intestine. All together, they are called the digestive system. The job of the digestive system is to change food into useful nutrients that can be used by your body.

Digestion begins even before you eat. When you smell delicious food, saliva, or spit, starts to form in your mouth. When you chew, you mix the food with saliva. Your tongue helps push the food around while your teeth chew. Chewing breaks food into small pieces and saliva breaks down the chemicals in food, so the food is now easy to swallow.

Next, food is swallowed and passes through the esophagus, a tube that leads to the stomach. Food does not just fall through the esophagus. Muscles in the esophagus slowly squeeze food down to the stomach. The stomach is like a mixer. It churns together all of the small pieces of food until they become even smaller. The food is broken down by digestive juices and strong muscles in the walls of the stomach.

When the food is ready to leave the stomach, it moves into the small intestine. Your small intestine is a long, winding, narrow tube packed inside you, just below your stomach. In an adult, the small intestine is about 22 feet long! The rest of the digestive process takes place here as the small intestine breaks down the food mixture even more. Food may stay in your small intestine for as long as four hours.

When food is completely digested, it is ready to be absorbed by the blood and carried throughout the body. Then all the important nutrients in food, such as vitamins, minerals, proteins, carbohydrates, and even fats, provide you with energy and strength. The leftover waste, parts of food that your body cannot use, go on to the large intestine and then leave your body.

Your digestive system is an important part of your body. It helps you get the nutrients you need to stay healthy and grow. The next time you sit down for breakfast, you'll know exactly where your food goes!

Before Reading

- What is the digestive system?
- How does your body get the nutrients it needs?

During Reading

- What organs are part of the digestive system?
- What are the steps of digestion?

After Reading

- What type of food may require more chewing?
- How is the stomach like a mixer?

Vocabulary

organ: a part of the body with a specific job

nutrient: things that help the body grow and stay healthy

churn: to stir or mix violently

absorb: to soak up; to take in

Identify Sequence

Sequence is the order in which something happens in a story. Clue words may be given to help identify sequence, such as **first**, **next**, **then**, and **last**.

The steps of digestion are described below. Put the steps in the correct sequence by ordering the steps from one to seven.

_____ Partly digested food moves into the small intestine.

_____ Food is chewed into small pieces and mixed with saliva.

_____ Nutrients are absorbed by the blood and carried throughout the body.

_____ Saliva starts to form in the mouth.

_____ Food is churned, mixed with digestive juices, and broken down further.

_____ Digestion is completed in the small intestine.

_____ Muscles squeeze food down the esophagus into the stomach.

Develop Vocabulary

Some stories have words that you may not know. Often, the meaning of a word will be explained in the sentence. You can understand the meaning of the word by reading the entire sentence.

Look for the following words in the text. Read the sentences containing the vocabulary words. Write the meanings given in the story. Then look up the words in the dictionary and give the dictionary meanings. Compare the two meanings.

Word	Meaning
saliva	Story meaning: Dictionary meaning:
nutrients	Story meaning: Dictionary meaning:
esophagus	Story meaning: Dictionary meaning:
small intestine	Story meaning: Dictionary meaning:

Comprehension Practice

Circle the letter of the correct answer.

1. What is the name of the body system that breaks down food into nutrients?
   A. muscular system
   B. skeletal system
   C. digestive system
   D. nervous system

2. How is the stomach like a mixer?
   A. It churns.
   B. It digests.
   C. It chews.
   D. It swallows.

3. In which organ is digestion completed?
   A. the small intestine
   B. the large intestine
   C. the stomach
   D. the esophagus

4. How does the body receive nutrients?
   A. Nutrients are passed back up into the stomach where they are absorbed.
   B. Nutrients are squeezed down the esophagus by muscles.
   C. You need to take vitamins to get nutrients.
   D. Nutrients are absorbed by the blood and carried throughout the body.

5. Which of the following words means a part of the body with a specific job?
   A. absorb
   B. organ
   C. churn
   D. saliva

One Boy's Wish Upon a Star

Before Reading

- Have you ever wished upon a star at night?
- If you were given a wish, what would it be?

During Reading

- What happened right after Bobby saw the star and made a wish?
- What did Bobby wish for?

After Reading

- Where did the fairy take Bobby?
- Who did Bobby pretend to be?

As Bobby was preparing for bed, he glanced out his bedroom window. Looking up at the night sky, he saw a multitude of stars and noticed one star that was brighter than all the others. Bobby gazed at that special star and made a wish.

Suddenly, he saw a ball of bright light speeding toward his window. The light entered his room, and in a flash, the ball turned into a fairy dressed in a dazzling white gown.

"Hello, Bobby," said the fairy. "I know that you have been a very good boy, and I am here to make your wish come true!"

Bobby's eyes opened wide in disbelief. Everything had happened so quickly that he was afraid to trust what he was seeing. Had that ball of light actually come down from the sky? Was that really a fairy standing in his bedroom? When she took Bobby's hand, he knew it was real. And before he even had time to think, out they went through the window.

As they soared higher and higher, Bobby felt a gentle breeze against his skin. He became aware of the brisk night air as he looked down and saw his house becoming smaller and smaller.

Before long, they arrived on a special island, and the fairy gave Bobby simple instructions. She told him that he could pretend to be anything he wanted in this extraordinary place—he only had to think it, and it would happen! First, Bobby became a valiant knight who saved a beautiful princess from a dragon. Then he was a pirate, looking for hidden treasures. He also pretended to be a superhero who saved the world from an evil villain.

Several exciting hours passed with Bobby imagining himself as different characters. When it was time to leave, the fairy placed a ball of light in his hands.

"You can return to this amazing place and continue your adventure whenever you want. Just take this ball in your hands, close your eyes, dream of returning here, and gently blow on the light. Your wish will be granted," said the fairy.

Before he knew what had happened, Bobby was back in his bedroom. He took the ball of light and placed it gently in a glass jar on his dresser. As Bobby fell asleep, he thought about all of the exciting adventures waiting for him.

Vocabulary

multitude: a very large number

valiant: brave

dazzling: very bright; sparkling

disbelief: the act of not believing something

villain: the bad character in a story

Identify Story Elements

There are three main parts of a story. **Plot** is what happens in the story. **Characters** are the people and the animals involved in the story. **Setting** is when and where the story takes place. Being able to identify the story elements will help you better understand what took place in the story and why certain events may have happened to the characters.

Complete the chart by identifying the story elements.

Elements	In the Story
Plot	What happened:
Characters	Who is involved:
Setting	When/Where it happened:

Analyze Characters

Characters are the people or animals involved in a story. Traits or descriptions of the characters may be revealed in the story by what the characters do or say.

Answer the following questions as you reflect on the story.

1. Why did the fairy come to answer Bobby's wish?

_____

_____

2. Bobby pretended to be a valiant knight who saved a princess from a dragon. What does this say about Bobby?

_____

_____

_____

3. Bobby was also a pirate, looking for hidden treasures. What does this say about Bobby?

_____

_____

_____

4. Bobby pretended to be a superhero who saved the world from an evil villain. What does this say about Bobby?

_____

_____

_____

5. Overall, what personality or character traits best describe Bobby?

_____

_____

_____

Comprehension Practice

Circle the letter of the correct answer.

1. What did Bobby do before he went to bed?
   A. He brushed his teeth and washed his face.
   B. He gazed at the stars using his telescope.
   C. He made a wish while looking at a star.
   D. He looked for the Big Dipper.

2. Where did the fairy take Bobby?
   A. to an amusement park
   B. to a special island
   C. to a pirate ship
   D. to a castle

3. Which of the following is an adventure that Bobby did NOT experience?
   A. being a knight fighting a dragon
   B. being a superhero saving the world
   C. being an astronaut walking on the moon
   D. being a pirate looking for hidden treasures

4. Which word could you use to describe something that is very bright?
   A. disbelief
   B. valiant
   C. dazzling
   D. villain

5. Which scene would Bobby most likely dream about himself?
   A. helping a little dog to swim across a river
   B. getting a puppy for his birthday
   C. spending time with his family at an amusement park
   D. learning how to drive a car

Is It a Kiwi or a Kiwi?

What comes to mind when you hear the word kiwi? You probably think of the kiwi fruit with its fuzzy brown skin. The kiwi is a leading New Zealand fruit. People enjoy the delicious green pulp and soft black seeds inside. Kiwi fruit is full of vitamin C and has a juicy, sour taste. Have you ever wondered where the kiwi fruit got its name?

Kiwi fruit is named after a New Zealand bird, also called kiwi, that has a similar appearance. Like the fuzzy brown kiwi fruit, the kiwi bird has furry, light brown feathers. The kiwi bird's body is somewhat round and stocky, similar to the egg shape of a kiwi fruit.

The kiwi is a bird that cannot fly because its wings are small and made up of only a few stiff feathers. A kiwi is about the size of a chicken, with two short legs and no tail. It has a long flexible bill and a short neck. The kiwi is the only bird that has nostrils at the tip of its bill. These nostrils give the kiwi an excellent sense of smell.

Kiwis live in New Zealand's wet forests but are rarely seen because they are so shy. However, the kiwi bird's call can usually be heard an hour before dawn and an hour after dusk. Kiwis have a tendency to avoid people when they are approached. They are nocturnal birds, which means they sleep during the day and are active at night. However, kiwis have poor vision, which makes them different from other nocturnal birds. At night, kiwis come out and use their exceptional sense of smell to find food. Kiwis use their bills to dig in the dirt to find earthworms and insects and to find berries.

A kiwi's brown feathers help it blend in with its environment, which is another reason why kiwis are heard more than seen. They dig their nests in the ground, and moss and ferns grow around the openings. A female kiwi usually lays one or two eggs. But it is the male kiwi that sits on them until they hatch, which usually takes about 80 days.

The kiwi is the national symbol of New Zealand and its people. But the kiwi is in danger. Two hundred years ago there were millions of kiwi living in New Zealand; today there are only about 70,000. Throughout New Zealand, groups of people are working to save this unique and remarkable bird.

Before Reading

- Have you ever tasted kiwi fruit?
- What do you imagine a kiwi bird looks like?

During Reading

- Where does the kiwi bird live?
- In what ways are the kiwi bird and the kiwi fruit similar?

After Reading

- Why are kiwi birds seldom seen by people?
- Why are there fewer kiwis now than two hundred years ago?

Vocabulary

stocky: strong looking, but usually short

flexible: able to bend without breaking

dawn: the first sign of sunlight in the sky at the beginning of a day

dusk: the time of day just before the sky becomes dark

Summarize and Paraphrase

After reading the text, you should be able to summarize the story. A summary is picking out the main points of a story.

Use the answers to the following questions to help you write a summary of the selection.

1. What are kiwi birds?

_____

_____

2. Where do kiwi birds live?

_____

_____

3. What are the kiwi bird's physical features, such as size, color, and shape?

_____

_____

4. How do kiwi birds find food, and what do they eat?

_____

_____

_____

Write your summary here:

_____

_____

_____

_____

_____

_____

_____

_____

_____

Ask Questions

Reread the story. Stop and think of questions about kiwis that you would like answered. Two questions are given for you to answer. Then think of, and answer, three of your own questions.

What I Want to Know About Kiwis . . .

1. Question: Why is kiwi fruit named after the kiwi bird?

    Answer: _____

2. Question: What makes the kiwi bird different from other birds?

    Answer: _____

3. Question: _____

    Answer: _____

4. My Question: _____

    Answer: _____

5. My Question: _____

    Answer: _____

Comprehension Practice

Circle the letter of the correct answer.

1. When is the call of a kiwi bird usually heard?
    A. before dusk
    B. after dusk
    C. when the male is sitting on an egg
    D. while the female is hunting for food

2. What is similar about the kiwi fruit and the kiwi bird?
    A. their fuzzy outer layer and brownish color
    B. their black dots
    C. their feathers
    D. their green pulp

3. Which of the following statements is NOT true of most nocturnal birds?
    A. They have good vision.
    B. They hunt at night.
    C. They cannot fly.
    D. They sleep during the day.

4. Which word describes a kiwi's bill?
    A. stiff
    B. fuzzy
    C. stocky
    D. flexible

5. What is one feature of the kiwi bird that helps keep it safe?
    A. the color of its feathers
    B. its unusual call
    C. its exceptional sense of smell
    D. the shape of its body

It Starts With You!

The bell rang to signal the end of recess. As Amanda started walking toward the door, she saw Daniel throw a gum wrapper on the ground.

"Daniel, I saw what you did! Why did you have to litter? The trash can is not even a foot away!" snapped Amanda.

"Come on, it's no big deal. It's just a gum wrapper. Plus, someone else will pick it up," complained Daniel.

"Just a gum wrapper? What do you think would happen if everyone in our school threw a gum wrapper or a soda can on the ground? Our playground would be full of litter! Wouldn't it seem like a big deal then?" questioned Amanda.

Amanda's words made Daniel stop and think for a minute. He imagined how the playground would look with hundreds of gum wrappers and soda cans on the ground. He pictured them in the sandbox, around the swings and monkey bars, and under the slides.

"Amanda, you're right! The playground would look awful, and it wouldn't be sanitary. It would be gross for the younger kids to find gum wrappers in the sandbox, and it wouldn't be safe to play soccer if we were stumbling over soda cans," said Daniel.

"You see, Daniel, the problem is that too many people think that someone else will do their work for them. People who litter assume that there will always be someone else to clean up the mess—or maybe they just don't care! But each one of us can make a difference at school and in our community. Keeping the school playground clean can start with just one or two people. Hopefully, our friends will see us as examples, and they'll stop and think before they throw their garbage on the ground. Maybe before too long, everybody in school will care," said Amanda.

"I never thought that one person could make a difference, but look how quickly you convinced me not to litter. I guess if we team up and encourage other kids to think about keeping our community cleaner, then we could make a difference," added Daniel.

"Exactly, Daniel! Change has to start somewhere, and it looks like it's starting with you!"

Before Reading

- Have you ever littered or seen someone litter?
- What would happen if litter piled up for days, months, or years?

During Reading

- Why did Daniel throw his gum wrapper on the ground?
- How could litter affect the safety of students at schools?

After Reading

- How can one person make a difference in a school or community?
- What could you do to clean up your school or community?

Vocabulary

signal: a sign

snap: to say something in anger

sanitary: clean and free from germs

stumble: to trip over something when walking or running

Use Prior Knowledge and Make Connections

Answer these questions about the selection.

1. What is the subject of this selection?

   _____

2. Have you ever had a friend tell you that you were doing something wrong? Did you become angry or did you listen to your friend?

   _____

   _____

3. When and where have you been guilty of littering?

   _____

   _____

4. When have you gone out of your way to keep your school or community clean?

   _____

   _____

5. Have you tried to set a good example for your friends or the younger students in school?

   _____

   _____

Identify Cause and Effect

Answer the following questions about cause and effect. Remember that a **cause** is why something happened and an **effect** is what happened. Answer each question below and then tell whether your answer is a cause or an effect. An example has been done for you.

1. What happened when the bell rang?

   Example Answer: Amanda started walking towards the door. (Effect)

2. Why did Amanda snap at Daniel?

   _____

3. Why did Daniel imagine the playground covered with litter?

   _____

4. What would make it dangerous for students to play on the playground?

   _____

5. What might happen if one person sets a good example?

   _____

Comprehension Practice

Circle the letter of the correct answer.

1. Why did Amanda snap at Daniel?
   A. He asked her to pick up his gum wrapper.
   B. She was angry because he littered.
   C. She tripped on a soda can.
   D. He gave her a piece of gum.

2. Why did Daniel think that throwing a gum wrapper on the ground was okay?
   A. Someone else will pick it up.
   B. Gum wrappers are not dirty.
   C. Everyone else does it.
   D. There was no trash can near him.

3. Which word describes something that is clean and free of germs?
   A. stumble
   B. signal
   C. litter
   D. sanitary

4. What did Daniel think was dangerous about empty cans on the playground?
   A. Young children would find them in the sandbox.
   B. They were not sanitary.
   C. Someone might trip on them.
   D. They might harm someone on the slide.

5. How can one person make a difference in the community?
   A. One person can do all the work in the community.
   B. One person can set a good example for others to follow.
   C. One person can make a public announcement.
   D. One person can give orders to the people in the community.

When Is a Bear Not a Bear?

The koala is a small Australian mammal that looks a bit like a cute little teddy bear. Even though koalas are called koala bears, or native bears, they are not actually bears. In fact, koalas are not even related to bears!

A Furry Animal: The koala has a big nose and big ears but no tail. Its fur is soft and thick and acts like a raincoat to keep moisture, or wetness, off. The fur is brown or gray on the koala's back and changes color with the seasons to act as camouflage. A koala has white fur on its belly. Koala fur is different in different parts of Australia. For example, southern parts of the country have very cold winters, so the koalas that live there have long shaggy fur that will keep them warm.

A Baby's Home: Like the kangaroo, the koala is a marsupial. The female koala holds her baby, which is called a joey, in a pouch. Female koalas have only one baby at a time, and the baby lives in its mother's pouch for about seven months. After that, the joey rides on its mother's back until it is about a year old. When a joey is first born, it looks like a pink hairless jellybean. A newborn joey cannot see or hear because its eyes and ears are still closed.

Food and Shelter: The koala spends most of its life in tall eucalyptus trees and only comes down to move to another tree. Koalas have sharp claws, long toes, and two thumbs on their front paws. Koalas are nocturnal, which means they sleep during the day and move around and look for food at night. Koalas eat the leaves and buds of the eucalyptus tree and don't normally need to drink water.

Keeping Koalas Safe: Koalas used to be hunted for their fur and were endangered. Now, there are laws to protect them. However, the number of koalas is still going down, since they are killed by foxes, dogs, cars, and diseases. Other dangers to koalas are forest fires and people. Trees are being cut down, and koalas are losing not only their homes but their food. Only about 100,000 koalas remain in Australia because most of their habitat has been lost. It is important to keep koalas safe so that the world can continue to enjoy these loveable native bears.

Before Reading

- What is a koala bear?
- Where do koalas live?

During Reading

- Where does a mother koala keep her baby?
- What is the koala's only source of food?

After Reading

- How does a koala's fur protect it?
- In what ways are koalas in danger?

Vocabulary

mammal: a class of animals with backbones and fur whose mothers produce milk for their babies

camouflage: something that blends in with its surroundings

shaggy: thick and bushy

habitat: the natural home of a plant or animal

Make Inferences

When you make an inference, you use reasoning and information that you already know to come to a conclusion. The answers to the following questions are not stated in the selection, but you can use inference to answer them.

1. What are marsupials? Thinking about how kangaroos and koalas are similar will help you infer what marsupials are.

_____

2. Why do koalas need sharp claws and two thumbs on their front paws?

_____

_____

3. All living things need water to survive. How is it possible that koalas don't normally need to drink water?

_____

_____

4. Why are trees most likely being cut down in Australia?

_____

_____

5. Why would it be impossible for koalas to live in a desert?

_____

_____

Use Text Organizers

The headings in a selection are helpful before you read. They give you clues as to how a selection is organized and show topics that will be covered. After reading a selection, headings can help you locate information quickly.

Read each question. Tell what heading you would use to find the answer. Then answer the question.

1. What do koalas eat?

Heading:

_____

Answer:

_____

2. What are baby koalas called?

Heading:

_____

Answer:

_____

3. What color is a koala's fur?

Heading:

_____

Answer:

_____

4. Where does a koala spend most of its life?

Heading:

_____

Answer:

_____

5. What was a danger to koalas? What are dangers to koalas today?

Heading:

_____

Answer:

_____

Comprehension Practice

Circle the letter of the correct answer.

1. Which of the following is NOT a use for the koala's fur?
   A. to find food
   B. for warmth
   C. to keep wetness off
   D. as camouflage

2. What do kangaroos and koalas have in common?
   A. eating eucalyptus leaves
   B. no tails
   C. white fur on the belly
   D. pouches

3. Which best describes a joey at birth?
   A. large and strong
   B. white and wet
   C. tiny and helpless
   D. gray and furry

4. Which of the following means "sleeping during the day and moving around at night"?
   A. marsupial
   B. nocturnal
   C. endangered
   D. habitat

5. Which is NOT a danger to koalas?
   A. buds and leaves
   B. disease and forest fires
   C. cars and people
   D. dogs and foxes

The Three Rs

Do you drink milk or orange juice that comes in plastic bottles? Do you eat cereal that is packaged in a box? If you do, you can help save the environment by creating less waste! And you can do that by practicing the three Rs—reduce, reuse, and recycle. **Reduce** is to use less, **reuse** is to use things again, and **recycle** is to take old things and make them into new things.

Creating less waste begins with thinking about the packages your milk, cereal, and other things you buy come in. A package only needs to keep the product inside safe. Flashy packages just create more waste. When you have a choice, buy packages that are plain and recyclable. Another way to reduce waste is to say no to store bags. If you only buy one or two things, you could carry them home in your hands, or you could take your old plastic bags back to the grocery store to be reused.

There are many ways to reuse material. Be careful when unwrapping a present and try not to rip the wrapping paper. You could save it and use it again. Shoeboxes can be used to store letters or other items and cereal boxes can be used as cardboard to make school projects.

There are probably many disposable items in your home that you could use again, such as plastic cups, plates, and utensils. Plastic forks, knives, and spoons can be washed and used again rather than being thrown in the garbage. Most of them will last a long time.

Recycling happens when materials are made into the same product or new products. Making new items from old ones uses less energy and natural resources than making those same things from new materials. Plastic soda bottles are recycled and made into T-shirts, combs, and other plastic goods. Aluminum cans are used to make new cans, and an old phone book might become one of your new schoolbooks.

There is so much you can do with very little work, and your small steps will make a big difference. And just imagine how great it would be if everyone practiced the three Rs! Don't wait—start now!

Vocabulary

environment: things that surround you—air, water, land, plants, and man-made things

waste: things that are thrown away or released into the environment

disposable: meant to be used once and thrown away

utensils: tools used in the kitchen

Identify Main Idea and Supporting Details

This selection is about the three *Rs*—reduce, reuse, and recycle. Find supporting details about each one and write them in the outer boxes.

Reduce

The Three *Rs*

Reuse

Recycle

Develop Vocabulary

Use content to help identify the meaning of each word below. Write your meaning and then the dictionary meaning of each word as it applies to this selection. The last two words have dictionary meanings as both nouns and verbs. Write each of those definitions.

Selection Word	What I think the word means	What the dictionary says the word means
product		
aluminum		
natural resources		
utensils		
disposable		
package		noun: verb:
waste		noun: verb:

Comprehension Practice

Circle the letter of the correct answer.

1. Which is NOT one of the three *Rs*?
   A. reduce
   B. reuse
   C. repair
   D. recycle

2. Which of the following is an example of reusing?
   A. throwing aluminum cans in the recycle bin
   B. buying a toy in a plain box
   C. washing plastic forks and spoons
   D. carrying home a bag of pretzels in your hands

3. What can be made from recycled plastic bottles?
   A. a T-shirt
   B. a newspaper
   C. a phone book
   D. an aluminum can

4. Which word describes things that are thrown away or released into the environment?
   A. utensils
   B. energy
   C. disposable
   D. waste

5. Which of the following describes recycling?
   A. using less of a material
   B. making materials into the same or new products
   C. using a product again and again
   D. unwrapping a present carefully

   Teacher Created Materials, Inc.

Small Girl in a Big Town

Tuesday was a depressing day for Gloria. She was leaving her house, neighbors, friends, and school to move to a new home in the city.

"Do we really have to go, Mom?" asked Gloria sadly.

"Oh, Gloria! I'm sorry that you're so upset," replied Mom. "But I think that you'll like living in a city. Life there will be much more exciting."

Gloria did not find Mom's words very comforting. Gloria had never moved before. She had lived in a small town in a rural area her whole life, and she could not imagine living in a city. The only thing on her mind was how nervous she was!

As they approached the city, Gloria looked out of the window and noticed the beautiful skyline. She had never seen so many tall buildings before, and some of her fear was replaced by excitement.

"Mom, Dad! Look at those buildings! I can't believe how tall they are. Will we be living in one of them?" asked Gloria.

Mom and Dad nodded their heads yes, and a smile spread across Gloria's face.

Dad drove the car down the busy streets as Gloria took in all the sights. She saw a video store, a pet shop, a grocery store, a library, and a beauty salon. They stopped at several lights, and after making more than a few turns, finally arrived in front of their new home. And it was indeed a skyscraper!

They parked the car and rode up the elevator to the twenty-fifth floor. The first thing Gloria did when she went inside was to look out the window. The view was absolutely amazing! She saw other tall buildings, the rooftops of shorter buildings, parks, and even the school she would attend. Gloria imagined that she could see her old home in the country.

Saying good-bye to her friends had been difficult for Gloria, but she was looking forward to attending a new school and meeting new friends. She decided to have a good attitude and explore the unfamiliar city—it would be an adventure!

Gloria began to realize that even if you are unhappy or frightened, you can still try to make the best of things. It is all about your attitude!

Before Reading

- Do you live in the city or the country?
- Have you ever said good-bye to friends because they or you moved away?

During Reading

- Why was Gloria so nervous about leaving her old home?
- Why was Gloria excited about her new home?

After Reading

- What did Gloria see from the car window?
- What could Gloria see from the window in her new home?

Vocabulary

rural: an area outside of the city, in the country

approach: to move closer to somebody or something

skyline: the pattern of shapes made by the buildings against the sky

attitude: an opinion or way of feeling about something

Develop Vocabulary

When you read a story, there may be some words that you do not know. Study the following words.

Words	Definition
rural	found in or living in the country
suburbs	areas where people live just outside of a city
urban	of or relating to a city

Complete the sentences using the words in the chart.

1. _____ are areas that are not too crowded and where many nice houses are built.

2. In _____ areas, there are many tall buildings. The streets are packed with people and cars.

3. Many farmers live in _____ areas, where it is quiet and peaceful.

Look for the words **unfamiliar** and **unhappy** in paragraphs 10 and 11. **Un-** is a prefix. Prefixes are letters added to the beginnings of words that change their meanings.

Prefix	Meaning
un-	not; opposite of

If appropriate, write the prefix in the space provided to complete the sentence. If not, leave the space blank.

4. I did not recognize him because he looked _____ familiar.

5. I could use the machine well because I was _____ familiar with it.

6. Frowning is a sign of _____ happiness.

Visualize

In this story, Gloria moves from a rural area to an urban area. When she looked out of the window from her skyscraper, she was absolutely amazed. Visualize and draw a picture of how the view of the city may have looked from Gloria's window. Then describe it on the lines below.

_____

_____

_____

_____

_____

Comprehension Practice

Circle the letter of the correct answer.

1. Why is Gloria sad in the beginning of the story?
   A. Her best friend is moving away.
   B. Her family is moving to a new city.
   C. She lost her favorite jacket.
   D. She has to visit the dentist.

2. Which of the following is a description of a rural area?
   A. loud and noisy
   B. full of tall buildings
   C. quiet and peaceful
   D. crowded with many houses

3. What did Gloria see as they first approached the city?
   A. a lovely park
   B. the library
   C. several video stores
   D. a beautiful skyline

4. Which word best describes Gloria on the day she moved?
   A. nervous
   B. tired
   C. hungry
   D. relaxed

5. What is the lesson Gloria learned on her moving day?
   A. Good sleep is needed before moving day.
   B. Having a good attitude is important.
   C. Big cities are better than rural areas.
   D. New friends are nicer than old friends.

From an Egg to a Frog

Frogs are animals that live double lives. They are amphibians—animals that live both on land and in water. Frogs begin their lives in water and live on land when they mature. These changes are called a life cycle.

Frogs, like other amphibians, lay their eggs in water. Most female frogs lay hundreds of eggs at a time. These eggs are round and tiny and have a jelly-like covering that protects them.

A newborn frog is called a tadpole. When a tadpole hatches from an egg, it looks like a tiny fish with only a round head and a long tail. Tadpoles swim in water and, just like fish, use gills to breathe. The tadpole's shape changes as it gets older. After about five weeks, the tadpole begins to grow back legs, and a few weeks later, front legs start to develop. As the tadpole's legs grow, its tail gets smaller. A tadpole swims around to get food and usually eats plants, but some tadpoles eat frog eggs or other tadpoles.

At about twelve weeks, the tadpole's tail is almost gone, and it starts to look like a young frog. Changes are taking place inside the tadpole as well. Its gills disappear as lungs begin to develop. When its lungs are fully formed, the tadpole climbs out of the water to become a frog.

A mature frog has bulging eyes and strong, muscular legs that allow it to jump on land and to swim in water. Even though a frog is now a land creature, most frogs need to stay close to water to keep their skin wet because they also breathe through their skin. An adult frog eats insects and other small animals such as spiders and earthworms. Most frogs catch their prey with a long, sticky tongue. Because they only have teeth on their upper jaws, frogs swallow their prey in one piece.

There are many species of frogs, and they live everywhere on Earth except Antarctica. People around the world have myths about frogs—in Japan, frogs are symbols of good luck; some Australians think that frogs bring rain; and in many Chinese stories, the frog is a trickster or magician. No matter what you think about frogs, they have been living on Earth for almost 200 million years—they were around in the time of dinosaurs!

Before Reading

- Have you ever seen a tadpole?
- What does a frog look like?

During Reading

- What are amphibians?
- How do tadpoles breathe in water?

After Reading

- How do frogs catch their prey?
- How do the Chinese portray frogs in their myths?

Vocabulary

bulging: curving out

prey: an animal that is hunted by another animal

species: a kind or type

myth: a traditional story

Compare and Contrast

Answer the questions and fill in this chart to tell how tadpoles and frogs are alike and different.

		Tadpole	Frog
1.	What body part does it use to breathe?		
2.	What does it eat?		
3.	What body part does it use to move in water?		
4.	What body part does it use to move on land?		
5.	What does its tail look like?		

Identify Sequence

The life cycle of a frog is described in this selection. Write about each stage of the life cycle of a frog, starting when it is an egg.

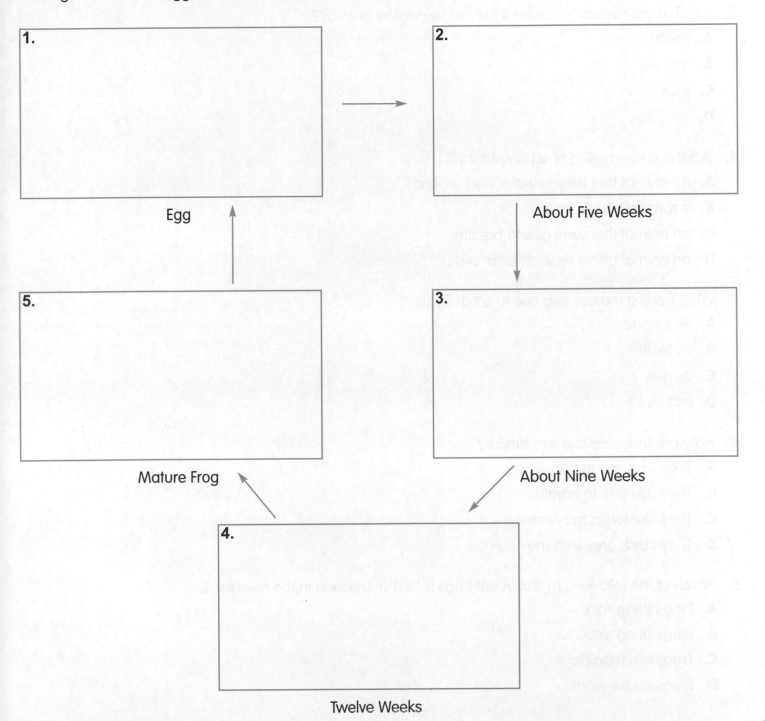

1.

Egg

2.

About Five Weeks

5.

Mature Frog

3.

About Nine Weeks

4.

Twelve Weeks

Comprehension Practice

Circle the letter of the correct answer.

1. Which word means "an animal hunted by another animal"?
   A. myth
   B. mature
   C. prey
   D. species

2. What is a description of an amphibian?
   A. an animal that lives in water and on land
   B. a mature female frog
   C. an animal that uses gills to breathe
   D. an animal going through a life cycle

3. What does a mature frog use to catch food?
   A. its tongue
   B. its teeth
   C. its gills
   D. its lungs

4. How are tadpoles and fish similar?
   A. They use legs to hop.
   B. They use gills to breathe.
   C. They use lungs to breathe.
   D. They catch prey with their tongue.

5. Which of the following myths about frogs is NOT mentioned in the selection?
   A. Frogs bring rain.
   B. Frogs bring good luck.
   C. Frogs are magicians.
   D. Frogs cause warts.

How Spring Came to Be

One day, the sun and the wind were arguing about who was better and more powerful.

"I am more powerful because I bring light and warmth to all plants and animals. The tiny flower buds wake up and unfold when they feel me rise. Without me, they cannot grow!" said the sun.

"I make things move from one place to another. I have the power to move boats across hundreds of miles of water and to carry pollen across the fields to ensure that new plants can grow. I am more powerful because, with a single blast, I can cause the flowers that you wake up to fly far away!" said the wind.

The sun and the wind went on and on, each trying to convince the other, and neither the stubborn sun nor the boastful wind would budge one bit. Finally, they decided to compete to discover, once and for all, which was more powerful.

"See that tree there?" the sun said. "We will see who can change that tree most." The wind agreed, and the competition began.

First, the sun gently warmed the leaf buds. The sap started flowing a little faster, and the tiny leaves burst out. What had been a drab gray branch was dotted all over with promising green. The wind took its turn then, gently blowing so that the new leaves danced, sending sunlight sparkling beautifully off the surfaces.

The sun burned a little hotter and the leaves grew rapidly until the tree was completely clothed. The wind continued growing stronger as well. The rustle of the leaves became a gentle, earthy tune. The moving leaves cast beautiful, ever-changing shadows in the cool shade of the tree.

The sun, not wishing to be outdone, became still hotter, beating down on the leaves and scorching them dry. Not to be outdone, the wind picked up, stripping the dry leaves and threatening the strong branches that were swaying in the strong wind.

The poor tree, its leaves suffering cruelly in the heat and its tired branches aching, had had enough! "Stop it, you two!" it cried. "You are both very powerful, and you are both very important. You don't need to prove yourselves. You, Sun, rule every summer. You, Wind, rule every winter. Can you not call a truce and be at peace for a while? Why don't you work together to bring soft warmth and light breezes for a gentle season?"

The sun and the wind thought hard about this. They did not wish to always be fighting. They agreed to a truce, and so spring was born. And the happy tree put out new leaves again to celebrate the season.

Before Reading

- What are the four seasons?
- What is the spring weather like?

During Reading

- How does the sun help flowers blossom?
- How does the wind move boats?

After Reading

- What is your favorite season? Why?
- Is this story real or make-believe? How do you know?

Vocabulary

ensure: to make sure about something

convince: to get someone to agree with you

stubborn: not willing to give in

truce: an agreement to stop fighting

boastful: proud

Classify/Categorize

Use information from the story and what you already know about weather to fill in the chart.

	Helpful Effects	Harmful Effects
Sun		
Wind		

Visualize

Good stories usually contain descriptions that help the reader "see" what is happening in his or her mind. Read the descriptions from "How Spring Came to Be." Underline the words that help you picture the scene. Then draw a picture in the space provided.

First, the sun gently warmed the leaf buds. The sap started flowing a little faster, and the tiny leaves burst out. What had been a drab gray branch was dotted all over with promising green. The wind took its turn then, gently blowing so that the new leaves danced, sending sunlight sparkling beautifully off the surfaces.	
The sun burned a little hotter and the leaves grew rapidly until the tree was completely clothed. The wind continued growing stronger as well. The rustle of the leaves became a gentle, earthy tune. The moving leaves cast beautiful, ever-changing shadows in the cool shade of the tree.	
The sun, not wishing to be outdone, became still hotter, beating down on the leaves and scorching them dry. Not to be outdone, the wind picked up, stripping the dry leaves and threatening the strong branches that were swaying in the strong wind.	

Comprehension Practice

Circle the letter of the correct answer.

1. Which of the following is NOT a character in the story?
   A. the sun
   B. the wind
   C. the moon
   D. the tree

2. What is one thing the wind can do?
   A. bring sunlight
   B. give warmth to plants and animals
   C. help plants grow
   D. carry pollen across fields

3. What is one thing the sun does NOT do in the story?
   A. scorch the leaves
   B. warm the tree sap
   C. blow off the leaves
   D. help the leaves grow

4. What did the tree say?
   A. Trees are more powerful than either sun or wind.
   B. The sun should come out in the day and the wind should come out at night.
   C. The sun and the wind could work together to bring gentle weather.
   D. The sun and the wind should draw territory lines.

5. How can this story best be described?
   A. as a biography, because it tells the true story of a person's life
   B. as a myth, because it is a made-up story that explains a natural event
   C. as a science article, because it explains how weather happens
   D. as historical fiction, because it tells a made-up story set in a real time and place

Keeping a Cool Head About Fire Safety

Sadly, many families lose their homes every year to fires. The causes of these fires vary. Sometimes electrical wiring gets too hot. Sometimes food is forgotten in the oven or a dish towel falls onto a burner. Sometimes people are careless with matches, candles, or cigarettes. Whatever the cause, home fires take families' homes, possessions, and sometimes even lives.

Heading Off Trouble: There are many things you can do to prevent fires in your home. Do a safety check with your parents. Make sure that all smoke alarms in the house work. Monthly tests are a good idea. Check to see that small appliances such as toasters are unplugged when not in use and that towels, potholders, curtains, and other flammable things are out of the way of the stovetop and oven. Look at electrical outlets and extension cords to ensure that they are in working order and not overloaded. If you have a fireplace, put a sturdy screen in front of it to keep sparks from coming into the room.

The Great Escape: Even with careful checks, fires can still happen. That is why it is important for families to have a fire-safety plan. First, plan two escape routes from every room in the house, if possible. That way, if smoke or flames are coming in one way, there is still another option. Second, agree on an outside meeting place like a tree or light pole so that everyone will know where to go. Finally, practice your fire escape plan at least twice a year. If your home has a second floor, make sure everyone practices, from a first-floor window, how to use a safety ladder to escape.

In the event of a fire, put your escape plan into action! Always check closed doors before opening them. If the door feels hot, use your second escape route. If the room is smoky, crawl on the floor. Smoke rises, so it will be easier to breathe lower down. You can also protect your lungs from smoke by covering your mouth and nose with a wet towel or piece of clothing. On your way out, don't stop to save possessions. It's much more important to save your life! After you have escaped, go to your meeting place and call the fire department. Once you're out, stay out!

A fire can be a scary experience, but being smart about fire prevention and having a plan for fire safety can save lives.

Vocabulary

possessions: things a person owns
flammable: that will burn easily
routes: paths

Before Reading

- What is the role of firefighters?
- What are some ways a fire could start?

During Reading

- What are some things you can do to keep fires from starting at home?
- Why is it a good idea to have two escape routes from a room?

After Reading

- Should you ever go back into a burning house for your possessions? Explain.
- Would you want to be a firefighter? Why or why not?

Safety Tip

If your clothing ever catches on fire, remember these three little words:

Stop immediately.
Drop to the floor.
Roll to put out the flames.

Use Text Organizers

Use the headings and other text features from the passage to answer these questions.

1. Why are headings useful?

   _____

   _____

2. Prevention means keeping something bad, such as a fire, from happening. Under which heading would you expect to find information about fire prevention? Explain how you know.

   _____

   _____

   _____

3. What information is given under the heading "The Great Escape"?

   _____

   _____

4. Different headings for the two sections might be "Fire Prevention" and "Making a Fire Safety Plan". How are these headings different from the ones the author used? Do you like them more or less than the ones in the passage? Explain your answer.

   _____

   _____

   _____

5. What information is included in the "Safety Tip" box?

   _____

6. Why do you think this information was put in a box separate from the passage?

   _____

   _____

Ask Questions

As you read a passage and after you have finished, you may have questions about the topic. Asking questions gives you goals for your reading and allows you to use the information you learned in the text to guide you to further reading that interests you.

Think of some questions you have about fire safety, how a fire department works, fire equipment, and more. Some questions are provided to get you started. You might find answers in the passage or from other sources. Then write three questions of your own and look for answers.

What I Want to Know About Fire Safety . . .

1. What are some common causes of house fires?

_____

_____

2. Smoke contains gases and materials that are very dangerous. Smoke inhalation, or breathing in smoke from a fire, can be deadly. What safety steps help you avoid smoke inhalation?

_____

_____

3. My Question: _____

_____

Answer: _____

_____

4. My Question: _____

_____

Answer: _____

_____

5. My Question: _____

_____

Answer: _____

_____

Comprehension Practice

Circle the letter of the correct answer.

1. What is a common cause of house fires?
   A. Food is left in the oven.
   B. Someone accidentally drops a match on a carpet.
   C. Old electrical wiring gets too hot.
   D. all of the above

2. What should you do in case of a house fire?
   A. Turn on an electric fan to blow out the flames.
   B. Get water buckets and try to put out the flames yourself.
   C. Leave the building immediately and call the fire department.
   D. Stop, drop, and roll.

3. When escaping a fire, why should you check a door before opening it?
   A. to make sure the fire is not too near it
   B. to make sure it is locked
   C. to avoid hitting someone on the other side of it
   D. to make sure you are using an approved escape route

4. What is the first thing you should do if your clothes catch on fire?
   A. Go to your family meeting place.
   B. Stop, drop, and roll.
   C. Stay low and cover your mouth and nose.
   D. Call the fire department.

5. If your house is on fire, what should you do before the fire department arrives?
   A. Go to your family meeting place and stay there.
   B. Go back in the house for your valuables.
   C. Practice using the fire safety ladder.
   D. Make sure all appliances are unplugged.

Life Among the Chimps

Before Reading

- What do you know about chimpanzees?
- How is a chimp like a person? How is it different?

During Reading

- What were some things that might have led Jane Goodall to have an interest in African animals?
- How did Jane Goodall earn the trust of the chimps?

After Reading

- What kind of personality or character traits does it take to move to another continent like Jane did?
- What is something you would like to study closer? What steps could you take to do it?

Vocabulary

predict: to guess something that will happen in the future

fossils: the remains of living things that lived long ago

warfare: the fighting between two groups that goes on over a period of time

groom: to clean

It isn't every day that a young scientist is offered the chance to spend every day with only chimps for company. But, then, not every young scientist would want such a chance. Jane Goodall was ready to go.

Goodall was born in London, England, in 1934. One of her first toys, a gift from her father, was a stuffed chimp. Who could have known that young Jane's toy predicted Goodall's life work? Jane was a curious girl, observing the animals and plants around her. Among her favorite books were The Story of Doctor Dolittle, about a doctor who could talk to animals, and The Jungle Book, about a boy who grew up in the jungle. Such stories began to plant an idea in Jane's head—a plan to live in Africa among the animals there.

As Goodall grew up, she began to work and save money to make her dream come true. Finally, at age 23, she went to Kenya and learned of the work of Louis and Mary Leakey. The Leakeys were famous scientists who had found many important fossils. Goodall met the Leakeys, and Louis Leakey invited her to join their team.

Goodall loved the work of hunting and studying fossils, but still she longed to study living animals. Louis Leakey had no problem talking Goodall into beginning a study of wild chimpanzees in what is now Tanzania. In July 1960, she arrived in Gombe National Park. She was to spend most of the next 25 years there.

It was difficult work. The chimps fled when she came near. Goodall had to patiently watch the chimps from a distance. But they allowed her closer as they got used to her. Eventually, the chimps let her follow them closely. They greeted her, sat with her, even groomed her—something that is usually done within a chimp family.

In her years of research, Goodall made discoveries that greatly changed the way that we view chimps. She learned that chimps act more "human" than was ever suspected. They hunt, use simple tools, conduct warfare, and adopt orphans. They have feelings much like we do. Young chimps tease, fight, and play games.

Goodall also saw how humans were harming chimps. She trained others to do the work at Gombe and began to travel to tell people about chimps. She wanted to teach them how to protect chimps and all animals. Today, Goodall speaks and teaches around the world. Her goal is to make sure her chimp pals are safe for a long time to come.

Identify Sequence

Sequence is the order in which events happen in a story. Put the following events in the correct sequence.

Goodall began to work with the Leakeys.

Goodall traveled around the world to speak about chimps.

Goodall saved money to go to Africa.

The chimpanzees slowly accepted Goodall.

Jane Goodall got a stuffed chimpanzee as a gift from her father.

Goodall met Louis and Mary Leakey in Kenya.

Goodall went to Tanzania to study chimpanzees.

Event 1:

Event 2:

Event 3:

Event 4:

Event 5:

Event 6:

Event 7:

Make Inferences

As a scientist, Jane Goodall had to use what she saw in the chimpanzees, along with what she already knew, to learn more about them. For example, she knew that mother chimpanzees take care of their babies. When she saw an adult female taking care of a baby that had lost its mother as though it were her own baby, Goodall concluded that chimps sometimes adopt babies and take care of them, just as humans do. This kind of thinking process is called "making inferences."

Use information from the article as well as what you already know to answer the following questions.

1. What part did Jane Goodall's parents play in her decision to live and work in Africa?

   _____

   _____

2. What can you tell about Goodall's personality?

   _____

   _____

3. Would Jane have begun her work with chimpanzees if she had not met the Leakeys?

   _____

   _____

4. Why did it take a while for the chimpanzees to warm up to Goodall?

   _____

   _____

5. How does Goodall's experience in Gombe National Park make her a good spokesperson for animal conservation, or efforts to protect animals?

   _____

   _____

Comprehension Practice

Circle the letter of the correct answer.

1. What did Jane Goodall hope to do in Africa?
    A. live among and study wild animals
    B. discover fossils
    C. write a book about the Leakeys
    D. buy a farm

2. Where did Goodall first meet the Leakeys?
    A. Tanzania
    B. the United States
    C. Kenya
    D. London, England

3. Where did Goodall go to study chimpanzees?
    A. Malaysia
    B. Tanzania
    C. the London Zoo
    D. Kenya

4. In what ways are chimpanzees similar to humans?
    A. They show emotions.
    B. They play games.
    C. They use tools.
    D. all of the above

5. What is Jane's goal now?
    A. to teach chimps how to make better tools
    B. to teach people how to protect chimps
    C. to turn Gombe National Park into an amusement park
    D. to find important fossils

The Festival of Colors

Family decorating each other for Holi Festival

I awoke on that spring morning with sunlight splashing through the little window near my bed pallet. My eyelids were still a little heavy. It had been a late night. But I could not help but smile, and I couldn't stand the thought of staying in bed another moment. This day was the brightest of the year, for it was the beginning of Holi—a festival held in northern India to celebrate the good harvest.

The air still smelled fresh and clean from the previous night's bonfires. Every family had contributed fuel for the fires. Sweet incense had been added, and the rich fragrance had filled the narrow streets and wafted in through open windows. The bonfires commemorate the mythical story of a wicked woman who tried to burn a young prince to death. He was saved and became a good ruler, but she perished. The fires of the night before were solemn business, but this day was different. No one could be serious at the start of Holi!

I was dressed in a flash but not in my new clothes. Mother would never forgive me if I had gone out in my new white cotton suit. My brother was waiting for me outside the house, checking his stock of gulal, or colored powder. Mine, I knew, was safely stashed in my knapsack. We set off in search of our friends. There was no trouble finding them, for there was squealing and giggling around the corner at one of the local fountains. Already our schoolmates were dripping wet, splashed in bright reds, greens, and pinks—and laughing uncontrollably. In short order, my brother and I too were colored for the season and joining in the chase.

We finally collapsed gleefully at the fountain to share the candy that is such a fun part of Holi. We heard music drifting over from the center of town, and we scrambled up to get there. We did not want to miss the folk dancing! I saw my father across the square. He had not escaped the gulal—splashes of red and green decorated his face and shirt. He caught my eye and gave a playful wink.

The dancing was followed by games and competitions for all ages. Even as this fun was going on, some of the teenagers were playing pranks and continuing the sneak attacks of water and gulal. The whole village seemed to be filled with laughter.

As morning passed into afternoon, we all returned home to clean up, enjoy a meal, tell stories, and rest. The quiet stillness of the late afternoon was a strange contrast to the craziness and color of that Holi morning. Still, it was a celebration to remember. I can hardly wait for Holi to come again!

Before Reading

- What are some traditions your family celebrates?
- What is your favorite way to celebrate a holiday or special occasion?

During Reading

- What is "gulal" and how is it used?
- Is Holi only a children's festival? How can you tell?

After Reading

- Why do communities celebrate events such as a harvest?
- Why do you think the Holi afternoon was quieter and more restful?

Vocabulary

pallet: a mat for sleeping

commemorate: to remember

solemn: serious

contrast: a sharp difference between two things

Identify Author's Purpose and Viewpoint

1. What do you think is the author's overall impression of Holi?

    _____

    _____

2. Stories are told from either a first-person point of view (meaning the storyteller is part of the action and uses pronouns such as **I** and **we**) or a third-person point of view (meaning the storyteller is not part of the action). What is the point of view in "The Festival of Colors"? How can you tell?

    _____

    _____

    _____

3. Read the two passages below. Decide which is told from the first-person point of view and which is told from the third-person point of view and circle the correct label.

Sonjay was dressed in a flash, but not in his new clothes. He knew his mother would be angry if he had gone out in his new white cotton suit. Sonjay's brother Arun was waiting for him outside the house, checking his stock of gulal, or colored powder. Sonjay knew that his was safely stashed in the knapsack at his side. The two boys set off in search of their friends.		I was dressed in a flash, but not in my new clothes. Mother would never forgive me if I had gone out in my new white cotton suit. My brother was waiting for me outside the house, checking his stock of gulal, or colored powder. Mine, I knew, was safely stashed in my knapsack. We set off in search of our friends.	
First Person	**Third Person**	**First Person**	**Third Person**

4. How are the two passages above alike? How are they different?

    _____

    _____

    _____

Identify Story Elements

Use the chart to identify the story elements of "The Festival of Colors." Answer the questions.

Story Elements	
Characters: Who is involved? What are they like?	
Setting: Where does the action take place? When does it take place?	
Plot: What is happening in the story? Is there conflict? How is it resolved? How does the story end?	

Comprehension Practice

Circle the letter of the correct answer.

1. What is celebrated at Holi?
   A. the prince's birthday
   B. the harvest
   C. the end of summer
   D. the making of gulal

2. What is traditionally done the night before Holi begins?
   A. People throw gulal on one another.
   B. Children stay at school late.
   C. Children go to sleep early.
   D. Bonfires are lit.

3. What is "gulal"?
   A. powdered dye
   B. a type of candy
   C. a traditional Indian dance
   D. a turban

4. Where does the music and dancing take place?
   A. by the fountain
   B. in the center of town
   C. at the narrator's house
   D. outside of town

5. What is NOT a traditional part of the celebration of Holi?
   A. throwing gulal
   B. eating sweets
   C. breaking piñatas
   D. folk dancing

Comprehension Review: Vocabulary—Word Meaning

Read each sentence. Use the information in the sentence to choose the meaning for the underlined word. Mark the answer.

1. Most frogs catch their <u>prey</u> with sticky tongues.
   A. animals hunted for food
   B. hunters
   C. plants used as food
   D. plant parts used to build homes

2. Serena was looking forward to <u>attending</u> a new school and meeting new friends there.
   A. waiting on
   B. giving care to
   C. applying at
   D. going to

3. Bats are <u>nocturnal</u> animals that sleep during the day.
   A. alert
   B. active at night
   C. hunting
   D. flying

4. Although a trash can was nearby, <u>litter</u> covered the ground.
   A. a group of young animals born at the same time
   B. stretcher
   C. scattered trash
   D. a basic metric unit

5. Gray, rainy days make me feel <u>glum</u> and lazy.
   A. happy
   B. enthusiastic
   C. gloomy
   D. agitated

Comprehension Review: Vocabulary—Opposites

Read each sentence. Choose the word that means the opposite of the underlined word. Mark the answer.

1. When a person is called a "silly goose," it means he or she is acting <u>foolishly.</u>
   A. happily
   B. wisely
   C. silly
   D. playfully

2. The <u>amusing</u> political cartoon in the newspaper made me smile.
   A. funny
   B. colorful
   C. serious
   D. witty

3. Talking back to your parents is <u>impudent</u> and unwise.
   A. rude
   B. discourteous
   C. unexpected
   D. respectful

4. The telegraph <u>transmitted</u> messages from one place to another over wires.
   A. wrote
   B. sent
   C. established
   D. received

5. We <u>separate</u> our recyclable paper and plastic into different bins.
   A. combine
   B. divide
   C. place
   D. remove

Comprehension Review: Vocabulary—Content Clues

Read each sentence. Use the information in the sentence to choose the best word to complete the sentence. Mark the answer.

1. We can see the _____ lights of a multitude of stars with the telescope.
   - **A.** nearby
   - **B.** blinding
   - **C.** distant
   - **D.** blue

2. The gills of a tadpole disappear as its lungs _____.
   - **A.** breathe
   - **B.** develop
   - **C.** shrink
   - **D.** overlap

3. A frog's _____ legs enable it to leap on land.
   - **A.** short
   - **B.** muscular
   - **C.** tired
   - **D.** front

4. Most cities do not have the large, open land that _____ areas have.
   - **A.** rural
   - **B.** metropolitan
   - **C.** urban
   - **D.** southern

5. For the environmental *Rs*, _____ means "to use less."
   - **A.** write
   - **B.** recycle
   - **C.** reuse
   - **D.** reduce

Comprehension Review: Sentence Completion

One word does not fit in the sentence. Use the sentence clues to choose that word. Mark the word that does NOT fit.

1. Kiwis cannot fly because of their _____ wings with stiff feathers.
   A. huge
   B. small
   C. petite
   D. tiny

2. Because he was _____, Roberto went to the library to do research on the topic of space travel.
   A. curious
   B. uninterested
   C. studious
   D. inquisitive

3. Finding food is one of the duties worker bees _____.
   A. perform
   B. have
   C. avoid
   D. accomplish

4. Receiving flowers was a _____ surprise.
   A. welcome
   B. pleasant
   C. nice
   D. terrible

5. Trains are used to _____ goods across the country.
   A. transport
   B. purchase
   C. distribute
   D. ship

Comprehension Review: Main Idea

Read each story. Mark the sentence that tells the main idea.

1. Homophones are words that sound alike but have different spellings and meanings. **Whole** and **hole** are examples of homophones. The word **whole** means "complete" or "entire." The word **hole** describes a hollow place.

   A. **Whole** and **hole** are examples of homophones.

   B. Homophones are words that sound alike but have different spellings and meanings.

   C. The word **whole** means "complete" or "entire."

   D. The word **hole** describes a hollow place.

2. The spring and early summer had been dry. The leaves of the cucumber plants were wilted. The tomato plants were not growing. These garden plants needed water to thrive.

   A. The spring and early summer had been dry.

   B. The leaves of the cucumber plants were wilted.

   C. The tomato plants were not growing.

   D. These garden plants needed water to thrive.

3. Squirrels are nutcrackers. They can use their teeth to open nuts. Beavers use their teeth to cut down trees. These two animals are rodents. All rodents can gnaw through hard things.

   A. They can use their teeth to open nuts.

   B. Squirrels are nutcrackers.

   C. All rodents can gnaw through hard things.

   D. These two animals are rodents.

4. Grains are an important food for people around the world. Asians grow and eat rice as a major part of their diet. Wheat used to make bread is a staple in many countries. Oats and corn are processed into many foods, including breakfast cereals.

   A. Asians grow and eat rice as a major part of their diet.

   B. Grains are an important food for people around the world.

   C. Oats and corn are processed into many foods, including breakfast cereals.

   D. Wheat used to make bread is a staple in many countries.

Comprehension Review:
Stated Details

Read the paragraph. Use the information in the paragraph to complete the sentences. Mark the answers.

When you think of tulips, you may think of the Netherlands, or Holland, as it is sometimes called. Tulips are an important agricultural product of Holland. Tulip farmers in the Netherlands produce almost 2,000 kinds of tulips. However, tulips are not native to the Netherlands. Tulips originally came from Turkey. In fact, the word **tulip** comes from the Turkish word for **turban**. A turban is a cloth headdress that looks like a brimless hat. The tulip was introduced to the European country of Austria in the 1500s. Europeans liked the flower a lot. Before long, the Dutch, as the people of Holland are known, and the English made it their favorite flower.

1. Tulips originally came from _____.
   A. Turkey   **B.** Netherlands   **C.** Austria   **D.** Holland

2. Tulip comes from a word meaning _____.
   A. mouth   **B.** turban   **C.** tunnel   **D.** pair of lips

3. Farmers in Holland grow about _____ kinds of tulips.
   A. 1,000   **B.** 1,500   **C.** 2,000   **D.** 2,500

4. A turban is a kind of _____.
   A. flower   **B.** agricultural product   **C.** country   **D.** hat

5. Europeans were introduced to the tulip in the _____.
   A. 1000s   **B.** 1200s   **C.** 1500s   **D.** 1800s

Comprehension Review:
Classify/Categorize

Read each group of words. Mark the word that does not fit in the same category as the other words.

1. **A.** bowl
   B. fork
   C. knife
   D. spoon

2. **A.** automobile
   B. truck
   C. airplane
   D. motorcycle

3. **A.** whale
   B. elephant
   C. kangaroo
   D. opossum

4. **A.** Jupiter
   B. Mars
   C. Earth
   D. Moon

5. **A.** noun
   B. verb
   C. object
   D. adjective

6. **A.** bean
   B. broccoli
   C. celery
   D. elm

7. **A.** town
   B. store
   C. village
   D. city

8. **A.** cub
   B. foal
   C. sow
   D. kitten

9. **A.** blankets
   B. beds
   C. covers
   D. quilts

10. **A.** river
    B. prairie
    C. pond
    D. stream

Comprehension Review:
Sequence

Read the paragraph. Then answer the questions about sequence. When you sequence events, you place them in the order they happen.

Making gelatin for desert or a side dish is easy. First, gather a bowl, spoon, measuring cup, and a box of gelatin. Next, put a kettle of water on to boil. Open the box of gelatin and put the powder in the bowl. Pour a cup of boiled water over the powder. Stir for about two minutes, making sure all the gelatin completely dissolves. Then, pour a cup of cold water in the bowl and stir. Next, place the bowl in the refrigerator. Now, choose some fruits or vegetables to put in the gelatin. For example, peel and slice some bananas or peel and grate a carrot and an apple. You want the fruit to be suspended throughout the gelatin, so let the gelatin thicken before you add it. Before it is completely set, remove the gelatin from the refrigerator and stir the fruit or vegetables into the gelatin. Finally, allow the gelatin mixture to set in the refrigerator. Later, you can serve and enjoy this tasty treat.

1. What do you put in the bowl first when you make gelatin?
    A. gelatin powder
    B. boiled water
    C. cold water
    D. fruit

2. When do you put boiling water into the gelatin?
    A. before adding the gelatin
    B. after adding cold water
    C. after adding fruit
    D. before adding cold water

3. What do you do to a banana before you add it to the gelatin?
    A. wash and peel it
    B. peel and slice it
    C. peel and grate it
    D. wash and slice it

4. Tell the order in which ingredients are added to the gelatin.
    A. cold water, fruit, hot water
    B. fruit, hot water, cold water
    C. hot water, cold water, fruit
    D. hot water, fruit, cold water

Comprehension Review: Plot, Setting, Characters

Read the selection. Use the information to answer the questions. Mark the answers.

Monday Morning Mishaps

Like every Monday morning, Barbara grabbed her backpack and rushed for the bus. That morning in May, she was even later than usual. She flew down the street and ran right into Justin, only the coolest boy in school. Books, pencils, calculators, and papers spilled out of their dropped backpacks. Justin mumbled something about watching where she was going, but he helped her pick up her things. Okay, she recovered from that, but as she got off the bus, she tripped. Her attempts to keep her balance plunged her right into Justin, who grabbed her and helped her stay upright. She thanked him, but he just waved her off. Wouldn't you know it? This was the day that her locker would stick. She pulled hard, and you guessed it. As it finally came open, she was thrust backward right into Justin. Justin laughed and said, "You, again! Why are you after me?" Barbara turned red. That night Barbara was sitting on the bus when Justin got on. Justin sat next to her and said, "I'm glad to see you're sitting down. It makes me feel safer." They both laughed, and they've been best friends ever since.

1. Where does the story take place?
    A. at home
    B. school bus and school
    C. in the library
    D. in a classroom

2. When does the story take place?
    A. Monday
    B. Saturday
    C. yesterday
    D. last night

3. Who is the main character?
    A. bus driver
    B. Justin
    C. Barbara
    D. the coolest boy in school

4. What does Barbara do at the beginning of the story?
    A. opens her locker
    B. trips as she gets off the bus
    C. sits on the bus
    D. runs into Justin

5. How does the story end?
    A. Justin stays away from Barbara.
    B. Barbara apologizes to Justin.
    C. Barbara and Justin become best friends.
    D. Barbara decides to never talk to Justin again.

Comprehension Review:
Predict

Read each paragraph. Use the information to predict what will happen. Mark the answers.

1. Cass has a favorite shirt with red buttons. Today, one of the buttons fell off as Cass was putting on the shirt. Cass found the button. She threaded a needle. What will Cass do next?

   A. throw the shirt away

   B. sew the button back on

   C. pin the shirt

   D. buy a new shirt

2. Nicholas rode his bicycle to the library. He put the bike in the bicycle rack and locked it. He took his library card out of his bicycle pack. What will Nicholas do next?

   A. ride his bicycle home

   B. play in the park

   C. buy a book

   D. go into the library

3. Mia's report is due tomorrow. She typed the report on the computer. Then, she printed the report and read it carefully. She corrected some mistakes and changed some sentences. She made the corrections on the computer. Then, she did a final spell-check and printed out the final copy. What will Mia do next?

   A. spell-check the report

   B. throw away the report

   C. hand in the report

   D. rip up the report

4. Sometimes Charlie has a bowl of cereal and milk for breakfast. He especially likes oatmeal covered in milk. Sometimes he enjoys a bagel with cream cheese. Today, the family ran out of milk. What will Charlie have for breakfast?

   A. a bagel

   B. glass of milk

   C. oatmeal

   D. a bowl of cereal

Comprehension Review:
Make Inferences

Read the sentences. Use the information to make inferences. Mark your answers.

1. Sam had never seen such a tall animal before. The animal with brown fur patches had long legs, but its neck looked even longer. It could nibble on leaves that most animals couldn't reach from the ground. Sam's mom said it was the tallest animal on Earth. What animal did Sam see?

   A. giraffe

   B. elephant

   C. antelope

   D. zebra

2. Every year, moonflower vines twine in and out of the garden fence. The plant's white flowers open every evening and close in the sunlight. The blooms are open now. What time of day could it be?

   A. morning

   B. noon

   C. early afternoon

   D. late at night

3. Karen wanted to know if her favorite team won last night's game. She looked in the newspaper to find out which team won. She checked out how other teams did too. What part of the paper did Karen look in?

   A. the news section

   B. the comics

   C. the sports section

   D. the advertisements

4. It was a short hike from the parking area to the river, but the walk was great. Wildflowers were just beginning to burst into bloom. Ian saw a baby deer with its mother. The buds on the trees were bulging and would soon be small leaves. The whole forest seemed to be awakening from a long sleep. What time of year is described?

   A. winter

   B. spring

   C. summer

   D. fall

Comprehension Review: Cause and Effect

Read each sentence. Mark the cause or effect for the sentence.

1. The trunk in the attic was locked. What is the effect?
   A. We couldn't go in the attic.
   B. We couldn't open the trunk.
   C. We closed the trunk.
   D. We found a map in the attic.

2. I wear glasses for vision. What is the cause?
   A. I have trouble seeing things that are far away.
   B. My eyes are blue.
   C. The pupils dilate in the dark.
   D. I can see better without the glasses.

3. I left the tray of ice on the table. What is the effect?
   A. The ice froze.
   B. The ice cubes were in a glass.
   C. The ice melted.
   D. The table got hot.

4. No one heard the knock on the door. What was the effect?
   A. The telephone rang.
   B. Everyone went to see who was at the door.
   C. The door stayed open.
   D. No one answered the door.

5. I was awarded the first-place trophy in tennis. What was the cause?
   A. I lost the tennis championship.
   B. I won the tennis championship.
   C. I put the trophy in my room.
   D. I did not play in the championship.